Your CV
in English

Éditions d'Organisation
1, rue Thénard
75240 Paris Cedex 05
Consultez notre site
www.editions-organisation.com

Chez le même éditeur :

Yannick Aubry, *Guide pratique et juridique de l'expatrié*

Patricia Levanti et Joselyne Studer-Laurens, *Téléphoner en anglais*

Ulrich Schoenwald, *Correspondance commerciale français-anglais*

Bénédicte Lapeyre et Pamela Sheppard, *Intervenir dans une réunion en anglais comme en français*

Charles Hampden-Turner et Fons Trompenaars, *Au-delà du choc des cultures*

© Éditions d'Organisation, 2000, 2004
ISBN : 2-7081-3136-2

Marcus et Stéphanie HURT

Your CV
in English

Votre CV pour l'international

Deuxième édition revue et complétée

Éditions
d'Organisation

The images used herein were obtained from IMSI's MasterClips collection, 1895 Francisco Blvd. East, San Rafael, CA 94901-5506, USA and from Corel Gallery. The authors wish to thank them for the use of these images.

TABLE OF CONTENTS

INTERVIEWS

The authors wish to thank the following managers for the interviews they so kindly granted us. Their comments provided invaluable insight into the evolution of recruitment in Europe.

Interview # 1
Stephen Cronin, Executive Director, Group Resources, Xerox Europe, Marlow, UK (Introduction, page 15).

Interview # 2
Edgar Britschgi, Andersen Consulting, Recruiting Director, ASG, Frankfurt & Zurich (chapter 1, page 33).

Interview # 3
Carolyn Nimmy, Global Staffing Director, Cap Gemini, Barcelona, Spain (Chapter 2, page 51).

Interview # 4
Laurent Yvon, Vice President Human Resources Europe, Hilti Corporation, Liechtenstein (chapter 3, page 93).

Interview # 5
Philippe Gracia, Human Resource Manager, Auchan Hypermarkets, Poland (chapter 4, page 110).

Interview # 6
Valerie Robert, Human Resource Manager, Procter & Gamble, London (chapter 4, page 112)

Interview # 7
Jo Pieters, International Human Resource Management Consultant, Philips, Netherlands. Responsible for Coordination of Global MBA Recruitment (chapter 5, page 193).

Interview # 8
Veli-Pekka Niitamo, Head of Global Resourcing, Nokia Telecommunications, Finland (chapter 6, page 209).

Interview # 9
Margarida Faustino, Human Resources Manager at Johnson & Johnson LDA, Portugal (chapitre 7, page 242).

Interview # 10
Mary Clark, Assistant Director for Recruitment, IESE, Spain (chapter 8, page 248).

TO OUR READERS

Ce livre est en anglais !

Un bon CV international ne saurait être la simple traduction en anglais de votre CV français. C'est toute la réflexion qui sous-tend votre recherche que vous devez mener en anglais, afin d'arriver au CV « juste » et éloquent.

C'est pourquoi nous avons choisi de vous accompagner dans ce livre **en anglais**, pas à pas, de la formulation de vos compétences à la mise en page de votre CV.

Alors… have a nice trip !

Introduction

CV or Resume?

Throughout this book we have used the word CV instead of the American word Resume (pronounced Resumé). Although recruiters in Europe recognize the word Resume, most recruiters in Europe use the word CV for Curriculum Vitae, However, if you apply for a job with an American company, it would be better to use the word Resume.

A BOOK TO HELP EUROPEAN JOB SEEKERS WRITE ENGLISH CVs (RESUMES)

The new European job seekers

We have written this book for **YOU**

- **European business students and graduates** who are applying for summer jobs, professional internships, or your first, post-graduation employment.
- **Professionals** who are making a *career change* into a new industry after experience in a different one.

This book specifically targets your needs for writing CVs (*Resumes*) and letters that get you interviews and job opportunities.

You think 'international' !

You are people who are looking for jobs internationally or with companies that <u>are</u> international or that <u>will go</u> international!

The meltdown of borders in Europe in the last ten years has been accompanied by a great number of young professionals seeking jobs in countries *that used to be considered* "abroad". No country in Europe is 'abroad' any longer for a European. Once national companies have taken *European* positions, seriously expanding their operations across borders, and multinationals have increased their presence in all markets. These developments call for *European* candidates and *European* job applications with companies that are international, although their headquarters may be based in France, Germany, UK, etc. Your chance of making a career outside your country has increased greatly, just as your chances of working closely with other Europeans–even if you are based in your home country!

For all these jobs you will write your CV in *English*! An English CV and letter is now a must! Even if you are applying in your home country in your native language, **an English CV and letter should accompany your native language application**. They are the best testimony to your capability of thinking like an international professional in the early stages of your job-seeking. They show you are ready to be operational internationally.

12

A Book for Career Starters and Career Changers

Often career *starters* and career *changers* face the same problems when trying to communicate their abilities to a potential employer. They may have very little or even <u>no</u> experience in the field they are applying for! If this is your case, you should know that **recruiters will expect you to prove that you can do the job! This book is written to teach you how to prove your capability**. It aims at helping you 'relive' your own experience, in English, in a way that shows how you can be useful for the employer and demonstrate your potential for growth as a future manager!

THINKING AND WRITING IN ENGLISH!

This book had to be written in English for three main reasons:

1. **It is addressed to all job seekers in Europe**
2. **It aims at developing your ability to read in English and to operate in English**
3. **It aims at developing your ability to talk in English about yourself and what you can do.**

This book focuses on building your capability to analyze what you have done and then express it in a way that managers and recruiters – all over the world – will understand. **The stress is on self-discovery and expression, in international language**, of what you find during that self-discovery. Both self-knowledge and communication will have a great deal to do with your success in job-seeking and the management career that follows. Although the authors have run seminars on job-seeking with multinational groups for years, we have long felt that a self-learning method was needed to help graduate job seekers and professionals to work their way step-by-step through their experience and its communication. **This book is the outcome of that long-felt need for a self-learning method.**

We encourage you to go through the book page by page even if you feel you already know much of what is said in some of the chapters: throughout the book, you will be going through a thinking process about yourself, **'reliving' your past in English, not translating it**. Translating a native language CV into English is possibly one of the worst possible ways of expressing your accomplishments and skills.

You must write your CV directly in English. The lessons of this 'reliving' will become extremely important when you reach the writing stage, and **you will be picking up the English vocabulary at the same time!** Two traveling companions will accompany you on your trip:

- **summaries of the key points** at the ends of the chapters to make sure you understand the essential message.
- and a **native language translation of these key points** following you **as you work in English**.

THE IMPORTANCE OF MANAGEMENT THINKING

You will learn to write your CV in a way a manager understands. Through the many interviews in this book, **you will understand how recruiters expect you to talk to them.** You will learn to process your experience and learning from a management point of view. Management analysis techniques are referred to throughout the book. Using these techniques will improve your ability to analyze and structure problems as well as communicate objectives during your career. There is a strong link between your skill in CV-writing and your understanding of management!

We know that it is often difficult to make others understand how you have contributed to the achievement of the objectives of the different organizations you have worked with over the years. Communicating your contributions well is essential to your success! In our seminars, over the years, participants from all over the world have spent most of their time learning to analyze their own – and others' – accomplishments, exchanging ideas on the value of their actions, as if they were writing **managerial** job descriptions and assessments.

These seminars have pointed out the strong connection between the management analysis and English language skills. Content is as important as language. Both native English speakers and non-natives have benefited from the double management/language focus. The English native participants have often pointed out that, although they knew how to act, they did not always think, and thus write, well about it! This is why we feel that the double content of this book is an important asset.

THE AUTHORS

The two authors have both different and yet converging backgrounds. One works particularly in **Strategic Management and Management Skills Training**, and the other in **Inter-cultural Management and Language Training**. Working as a team in CV-writing and Job Search seminars, a happy marriage of the two skills sets occurred. In these seminars, we came to realize that understanding management was essential to CV-writing. We discovered that understanding one's skills and offering services to companies went hand-in-hand with management thinking and learning. This book is the outcome of some 20 years of teaching both CV-writing and Management.

INTERVIEW # 1:
AT XEROX WE RECRUIT ON A PAN-EUROPEAN BASIS

Interview with Stephen Cronin, Executive Director, Group Resources, Xerox Europe, Marlow, UK.

▶ **Has recruiting changed at all in the last few years at Xerox?**

Greatly. In the last two or three years Xerox, Europe has made major changes in its recruiting approach. It might be better to describe it as a pan-European 'resourcing strategy.' Pan-European means that we now tend to draw on an 18-country pool whereas we used to recruit locally. There is a very conscious effort to reach 'Euro-diversity.' Other changes have occurred within the framework of this pan-Europeanism: a stress on industry skills recruiting, the use of partnering in recruitment, and volume sorting.

• As our customers have become more transnational and the services they require more global, there has been a growing need for personnel with industry specific skills. Whereas we used to look for somebody with good 'generic' sales experience, regardless of the industry, we now seek out those with experience in handling specific industrial accounts. Generic skills as recruitment criteria have given way to area skills, coupled with industry knowledge. Successful applicants will bring in at least two skills sets, often two to three languages.

• Partnering has taken a key role in our management of the recruitment process. Xerox depends on multi-country search agents to ensure that recruitment secures the same profiles throughout Europe. Our role is to work out these profiles for the search agents. Xerox

Human Resource Management often works by projects. For example, right now we are seeking up to 100 Systems Integration specialists. In the profile we develop, we will not only include Systems Integration literacy, but also aim at 70% university graduates.

- The volume of applications to process has reached astonishing proportions. Third party agents may receive over 10,000 responses. Therefore, the criteria for sorting these responses needs to be very carefully worked out.

Accompanying this move to 'Euro-diversity' has been a conscious effort to increase the number of women and of university graduates in the company. Grads now make up 60% of our sales force. The percentage of women sales executives has grown from 5% a few years ago up to 25% today. The progression of women to positions in management committees has been similar.

▶ How have these changes affected the recruitment market?

It has become much more competitive. Despite the high volume of applications, there is a constant fight to find – and then keep – the right people. We no longer use a 'shotgun' approach, aiming at a broad population of candidates. Our highly focused skills search approach means we target people from the top 25 companies that we have benchmarked as excellent in the skills we are seeking.

▶ In light of these changes, for Xerox, what will make a successful CV?

In our business, the hard copy CV has declined seriously. Our headhunters tell us that 60 to 65% of applications will come over the Web. When we do receive a hard copy CV we write back to the candidate to apply through our search agents. In those CVs, three things will be looked for:

- Applicants' knowledge of an industry: if he or she has good skills in finance services or retailing, for example. Once with Xerox, they may make a lateral move into other industries, but they will be brought in for specific industry skills.

- The company they work for now: is it in the top 25 companies benchmarked as excellent in that industry?

- Their personal skills set.

This means that the chronologically organized CV is not very useful. We do not want to see a detailed 'list' of responsibilities, nor the number of people you had reporting to you. After information that shows applicants' industry knowledge and education, we will want to be able to identify what skills they bring to the business. Their accomplishments and contributions should be 'up front'. They should show what they have 'achieved,' not simply 'done'. They should show how they have used their skills. This is the "meat on the bones", so to speak. The cover letter in this process has become very unimportant.

Key points in introduction

- Write as CV in English for every job anywhere.

- You must learn to think in English and not translate.

- Think like a manager and you will write a good CV.

- Faites un CV en anglais quel que soit l'endroit où vous postulez en Europe.

- Apprenez à réfléchir directement en anglais et à ne pas traduire.

- Mettez-vous dans la peau d'un manager quand vous écrivez votre CV.

Difficulties in writing a CV

You are about to tackle one of the most difficult 'arts' there is. Yet it is an art that is directly related to life; it is certainly not "art for art's sake." It has everything to do with finding a way of making a living, of building a career. Learning to do it well will contribute to your management capability and success, because you will learn to focus your own and other efforts on the essential, learn how to analyze projects and formulate clear objectives for yourself and others.

Then, if CV-writing is so linked to the above skills, why does everybody seem to hate it so?

UNDERSTANDING WHAT THE CV IS FOR

Lots of younger job-seekers have trouble understanding exactly why they have to write a CV – older ones too! They don't believe it does much good and so they rush it off haphazardly. Since they don't understand what the employer is really looking for, they figure it is a game of chance; they roll the dice and see what comes up!

In this book, we have included a number of interviews with recruiters from European companies to help you find out exactly what recruiters expect to learn from a CV and letter. Actually recruiters hope to learn a great deal! They are on the look-out for a number of people who can bring in the skills they need to help move their companies along, and it would be very expensive to interview all of the applicants. Therefore, they are hoping that your CV and letter will provide enough information to make it possible to call you in for an interview and get to know you in depth. If you realize the utmost importance of providing the information they need to make an informed choice, you will have gone a long way towards writing a CV that does good for you and the recruiting company!

NOT KNOWING WHAT TO PUT IN THE CV

This goes hand in hand in understanding what it is for, but even when you do understand the purpose of a CV, you may still have difficulty choosing what to put in it, or how to lay it out! That is obviously what this book aims to coach you in. This book is organized to answer your questions in the following order:

- Chapter Two will explain what each part of the CV/Letter package does for you.

- Chapter Three will help you understand the company and yourself so that you can write a package that communicates!

- Chapter Four will tell you what to put in the CV.

- Chapter Five will show a number of ways of structuring the CV to suit both your particular case and the specificities of the job you are applying for.

- Chapter Six will give you some pointers on CVs to make your CV easy to read so that it shows what you want to show.

- Chapter Seven will develop your skills in writing a letter that really supports a CV.

- Chapter Eight is a special chapter that shows how your learning can be carried over to MBA applications. It is addressed to graduates who would like to pursue their studies in MBA programs in Europe or the US.

Lack of training leads to misconceptions about CVs

In our teaching over the years, we have asked students from universities all over Europe what kind of training they received in the building of CVs. With the possible exception of the UK, the answer was all too frequently: *none*! Only recently, in a series of interviews, we learned a number of interesting points:

- Students write CVs that are simple *lists* of activities because they "think" everybody does it that way.

- Often they have no idea whether the CV should be organized chronologically like a "history" or start with most recent events first.

- If training is provided at their institution, they seldom attend, feeling that it is more or less obvious what has to be done.

- Very often, when they write a CV in another language, they quite naturally go to their language teachers for help.

We can correct certain misconceptions linked with the above "approaches" right away.

- *First*, since companies are hoping to find out a *great* deal about applicants and are looking for information about your skills, a simple list of activities teaches recruiters nothing about you. A list CV leaves it up to them to "read into" the CV what it is really your responsibility to explain.

- *Second*, since a CV is an offering of skills to solve a company's problems and your most recent experiences should have permitted the greatest development of those skills, it is logical to talk about *now* before talking about *then*. Recruiters are not necessarily interested in history for history's sake!

- *Third*, it is typical of all of us to seek training only when we feel the need for it, and at our own pace, avoiding committing too much time to what seems obvious. If CV-writing or job-seeking seminars are offered, typically it is during a week when we do not feel like working on a CV. That is why we felt this self-study book would allow you to focus on what you want at your own pace. On the other hand, what is to be done is far from being obvious. And the CV is crucial in your job-seeking!

- *Last*, it is not disparaging to language teachers to point out that they focus on language rather than content and are often academics who are used to writing CVs more often suited to applying for jobs in the academic world than in the business world. In an academic CV, lists of publications are quite usual. On the other hand, in management, you are more likely to be expected to write project reports, which are not at all similar to lists. Project reports show actions taken and results obtained. Ask your language teachers for help certainly, *but first work out what to say and how to structure it on your own.* You must take the responsability for the *content* of your CV, and then ask your language teachers if it communicates clearly, language-wise.

DOERS ARE NOT NECESSARILY WRITERS

Another difficulty that arises in writing a CV is that, when we have a taste for "doing", we do not necessarily like writing. High achievers are not necessarily writers, and, even if so, they might like to write something else than a CV and a job application letter. People who go into business and management are often people who like focused action, changing situations and working with people. They also have a definite preference for the spoken over the written word. As Henry Mintzberg pointed out in his ground-breaking study of the Role of the Manager,[1] managers seldom read long reports and prefer getting their information orally. This is because oral information is interactive and allows the manager to ask questions, be selective and probe for more detail. Oral information is also richer because it includes tones of voice and gestures. Moreover, it is fresher, whereas yesterday's report, based on information from at least a week ago, is outdated.

This should remind us as well that business people do not like reading CVs any more than the applicants like writing them. Employers will have a definite preference for CVs that provide rich information, waste little of their time and almost seem interactive.

The frustration of writing instead of acting

This distaste for writing is widespread and often affects even those whose profession would seem to call for a lot a writing. Balzac, the great French novelist, hated writing and had to force himself to crank out a novel, often to meet a deadline with a publisher. It is said he had himself chained to the bed overnight so that he would have to stay inside and finish a novel. Many a doctoral candidate has never acquired his Ph.D. because he could not bring himself to write down and structure years of research. He liked the learning, but not the telling!

Underlying this distaste we often have for writing is the feeling that so much will be lost when it is put down on paper. How can we take the wealth of information about an on-the-job experience – with the

---

1. Mintzberg, Henry, "The Manager's Job: Folklore and Fact", *Harvard Business Review* (July-August 1975).

people who were working around us, the customers, the other workers and all the chaos of the moment – and hope to ram it all into a structure on paper that conveys anything like what we lived through?

The truth is that a great deal will indeed be lost! Writing requires choice. We cannot say everything, so the whole art becomes one of knowing *what to choose to say*.

There are several other problems that arise in writing a CV when you are a student, recent graduate or someone changing professions:

- The feeling that you have very little experience to show in the field you are applying for
- The dislike of being judged on so little information
- The difficulty in showing your worth
- The trouble of getting the employer to understand what you mean

An additional difficulty is added in applying at the European level:

- The problem of communicating transnationally a context you feel is specific to your own country

The feeling that you have very little experience to show

One feeling you have to overcome right away is that you don't have much experience. This is true when you compare yourself to a professional who has been in business for 20 years. On the other hand, what you must remember is what Aldous Huxley pointed out in *Brave New World*:

" Experience is not what happens to a man, but what he does with what has happened to him. "

Professionals might be able to write pages and pages of details on their experience, yet the employer will typically want to read a CV close to *one page in length.* [2] In the one page, the employer will want to see the learning accomplished by the applicant and the skills he or she has to offer. In a sense, the one-page CV gives the beginning, would-be professional an advantage over the more experienced applicant who has *too much to say.* If you are an experienced professional, your advantage will probably be that you have developed a talent for communicating the essential in management. If you are a career starter, on the other hand, what matters is what your life experience, school experience, or work experience has been catalyzed into.

The dislike of being judged on so little information

This difficulty is closed linked with the one above. *Yet, the one-page rule imposes a need for brevity on entry-level applicants and experienced professionals alike.* So, in a way, it balances the game out. The dislike of being judged on so little information is in no way specific to newcomers to the job market. Remember that in management, decisions on promotion or re-assignments may be based on the equivalent of one paragraph of text. This paragraph may sum up a variety of results attained by the manager in question. When you write a CV, you have the great advantage of being able to choose the information you wish to stress – in a sense you are writing your own performance appraisal! This is both an advantage and a challenge. Increasingly, companies are asking their personnel to write their own self-evaluations before having their performance appraisal interview with their bosses.

The difficulty in showing your worth

Convincing others of one's worth is a key talent for anyone who wishes to progress in the management world. So even if it is difficult, it is a skill that must be developed. A major step ahead can be made by recognizing your own worth and learning to express it in ways that others understand. A lot of it has to do with understanding what the others consider 'worthwhile'. Putting yourself in others' shoes can

---

2 See Interview with Valerie Robert, Procter and Gamble, Chapter 4, page 112.

help a lot. Work out what 'being successful' in a certain profession really *looks like* in terms of accomplishments. Then analyze your own accomplishments in those terms. If you do that, you will be successful in communicating your worth.

The trouble in getting the employer to understand what you mean

This, of course, is the whole point. You have to make the reader understand what you have really accomplished. Most of the difficulty comes from not really thoroughly analyzing for ourselves what we have done and relating it to the employer's value system. The rest of this book deals with just that: understanding what success in management *looks like*, analyzing what we have done and learning to communicate it like managers.

The problem of communicating transnationally a context you feel is specific to your own country

In the current context where truly European companies are being formed, it is becoming commonplace to apply across borders for jobs, or, at least, apply to a transnational in one's home country for a transnational job.[3] This process calls for a *European* CV. European graduates often feel that it is hard to communicate clearly what they have done, when they come, for instance, from Sweden and are applying in France.

Actually this poses few problems. All European students come from educational systems and backgrounds that are more linked by their similarities than they are separated by their differences. When applying to European or global companies, local differences should not be focused on. Instead, effort should be made to talk in universal terms; management values are tending to develop into a universally accepted value system in Europe, in the work place at least. You are not writing to explain the educational system in your country! On the other hand, it might be useful to stress the differences in your background, when knowledge of a certain country and its cultural specificities constitute a distinctive offering to an employer.

---

3 See Interview with Stephen Cronin, Xerox, in the Introduction, page 16.

CV-writing is closely linked to action

Many of the difficulties involved in CV-writing may be overcome if you realize that it is highly linked to action – your actions! *In fact, the only subject of a CV is your actions!* If well written, it is very positive because it focuses on actions you have taken in organizations which have led to other actions. Its backdrop is the real world in which people are transferring products and services, creating wealth, and leading change. In this sense, it is very 'hands-on' and very far away from the academic dissertations students have often turned out in large numbers in their educational careers.

Too often the communication skills developed at the university seem far removed from the needs of communication in organizations; academic writing style does not seem very related to the ability to communicate to fellow team members working on a project. *Yet, recruiters are glad when applicants have years of education behind them,* because they know that those applicants will have learned to structure complex information and acquired a range of vocabulary and ideas that enables them to deal with complexity.

Communication skills are crucial in modern management

In Western countries since WWII, organizations have increasingly moved away from 'command and control' structures which so typified business 'administration' for the first part of this century. Although, these kinds of structures are still often employed in Third World countries, even by multinationals of Western origin, in Western countries themselves 'tall' hierarchies have been played down in favor of flatter organizations, lateral teams and project management. With these developments, communication skills have come to the forefront of management, even in entry-level jobs.

More and more, recruiters stress that the two major kinds of skills they need from people arriving on the job market are project management skills and communication skills. Management itself is at least half communication! And project management requires an ability to fit a series of complex tasks together into the achievement of concrete outcomes – this is very different from what can be conveyed by a CV written as a simple list of jobs worked and courses followed! In writing your CV, you will learn to relive projects you have carried out and think about them like a manager.

CV-writing is a kind of management training

The relation between CV-writing and clear management thinking cannot be stressed too strongly! In writing your CV you will have to think like a manager about your past experience as well as about the organization you are applying to. As we move away from the 'command and control' organization, business *administration* is giving way to *management*; this means that as opposed to the previous 'top-down' flow of orders, empowerment at all levels is now calling for multi-directional exchanges of information. This might be called 'in-real-time feedback'. This necessitates a simultaneity in thinking which makes everybody a manager: employees must blend awareness of company business and strategy with project planning and carry-through capability, coupled with the ability to communicate objectives and job assignments clearly.

Your Organization and You

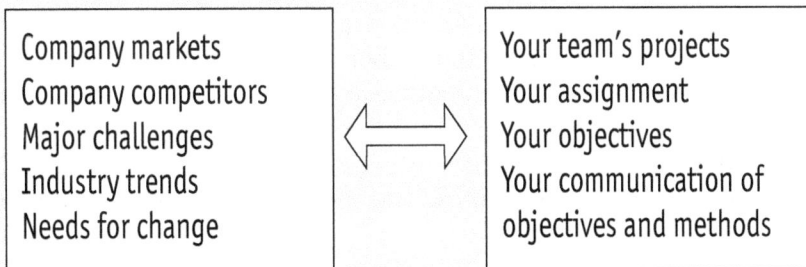

From the point of view of CV-writing, this blended awareness means that you must learn to understand an organization's business and strategy, learn to communicate objectives and your job assignments clearly and make the link between them.

Your organization and you

Company markets Company competitors Major challenges Industry trends Needs for change	⟺	Your team's projects Your assignment Your objectives Your communication of objectives and methods

Your Organization

To become a productive member of any organization, you should understand its markets, technology and the challenges it faces. As we move into the Third Millennium, ideas of 'strategic intent' in companies require the increased involvement of all employees in strategic awareness. In many industries, the speed of change is such that strategic information can only come into the firm only through the employees who are interfacing with customers and suppliers. Total Quality Management has already had two major effects in Human Resource Management: it has driven home the need for total involvement in processes by all employees, and it has enlarged individual's scope of responsibility. This means that complete knowledge about the organizations you have worked with in the past is essential for showing the level of commitment you felt.

A new definition of commitment is being written; commitment now means full involvement in the organization as a whole[4] – not in one department or in one project! It means caring about the firm's strategy, its markets, developments around it, and its needs for internal change. Showing a thorough knowledge of the company you are applying to is crucial for showing the level of commitment you are offering. It is also basic *politeness*!

When sifting through your own experience, the word strategy may seem relevant to an assignment you performed with a consulting firm or an export survey you carried out for a company, but might strike you as out of place when you are talking about working for a church, scouting, waiting on tables or washing the floor of a butcher shop. Yet it is not! As a management student, remember that recent history has shown that every organization needs to gain involvement from its employees. Remember as well that the scout group and the corner butcher shop all have strategies. Perhaps they are more simply expressed, in the first case, as passing values and training down from generation to generation, and, in the second case, as ensuring return business; but they are strategies nevertheless.

---

4 See Interview with Philippe Gracia, Auchan Hypermarkets, Chapter 4, page 110.

YOU

To show your involvement in the organizations you have worked with in the past or are working with now, you need to learn to communicate objectives and job assignments clearly. Only in this way will you be able to show the nature of your contributions to the organization. Revealing your understanding of the relationship between different activities and departments in an organization will have a great deal to do with the success of your CV and of your career! Chapter Four will deal with this in depth – in conjunction with systems thinking. Our experience has taught us that this is typically the most difficult part of CV-writing for students and experienced professionals alike. Above all, it takes work!

CV-WRITING TAKES WORK!

Our group seminars usually last some 20 hours. This is a major commitment of time from the participants who devote another 20 hours to writing on the outside. If you work your way through this book and quickly understand where you are going, and spend some serious time writing and bouncing your different drafts off friends, it should take you a full week to turn out a good CV and letter. This investment is one of the difficulties of CV-writing. However, other investments are riskier! Careful time devoted to this art will assuredly pay off in job offers, greater career success and greater ease in applying for jobs in the future as you move around in the business world. Moreover, *without* the investment, you are unlikely to get where you want to go to!

TELLING THE TRUTH

Ethics and job applications

Perhaps the last difficulty in CV-writing is telling what you feel to be the truth. Not because you have a tendency to lie! We have found most of our seminar participants to be extremely honest, to the point where they hesitate to use positive language. They have instinctively recognized the difference between *embellishment* and *lying*, but find it very difficult to master the borderline! Therefore, they tend to play down their real contributions for fear of using language badly and wind up telling a lie by minimizing their skills.

Americans have been taught to *positivize* their achievements. When they do this, it sometimes takes the form of 'hype'. In its more extreme forms, *positivizing in any country* can get out of hand and lead to exaggeration that borders on lying. In Chapter Four we provide a list of actions verbs that might be used in describing personal accomplishments in your CV. We have avoided verbs like 'masterminded' which we find phony. Such verbs portray a very 'puffed up' picture of an applicant, are hard to live up to, and, moreover, indicate that the person is far from being a team player.

Painting in very positive language what you have accomplished may seem necessary to open doors of opportunity, but may also put you in a position where you build your reputation on distortion of the facts. Others feel that "stretching" the truth is necessary to get an opportunity that might otherwise escape them. They tell themselves that, once given this opportunity, they will show they were capable of it all along. They conclude that taking the risk of lying was worthwhile. To be fair, it should be remembered that a number of careers in history have been started on pure nerve![5]

We are not going to get caught up in a debate as to what stuff careers are best built on – which is beyond the scope of this book – although we would like to think it is competence. In this book, we focus on helping you become aware of your competencies and communicate them to potential employers. We would like to suggest a few ground rules that should provide any of you with an approach to truth in job seeking that you can feel comfortable with.

---

5 In the US, recent reports say that 10% of applicants "seriously misrepresent their background or work histories, and that 30% of applicants exaggerate their accomplishments!" This has led to the rise of an important new business–reference checking. Increasingly, experts are being hired by U.S. companies, who want to hire truthful employees and avoid costly lawsuits arising from crimes committed by workers hired without reference checks.

INTERVIEW # 2:

AT ANDERSEN CONSULTING, WE NEED GOOD INFORMATION IN A CV AND A LETTER

Interview with Edgar Britschgi, Andersen Consulting, Recruiting Director, ASG, Frankfurt & Zurich.

▶ **Could you give us an overview of how Andersen Consulting recruits?**

Recruitment at Andersen Consulting is organized by geographic area. I am in charge of recruiting for Austria, Switzerland and Germany (ASG), essentially the German-speaking areas of Europe. Other managers handle France and Benelux, or the UK and Ireland, for example. My responsibility is to select, assess and carry through to contract. To find qualified applicants, we go to job fairs, organize recruitment events and also use search firms – but only at the executive level. Andersen Consulting has a very high rate of growth, roughly 20% a year, and we need a lot of new people just to keep up with that growth – not to mention a small number of replacement staff. All in all, we hire about 800 new people a year – plus replacements!

We seek two types of profiles: 1) process and technologically skilled people, engineers, and computer software and systems people make up about two thirds of our recruits, 2) strategy and change management people represent about one third. For our younger recruits we maintain a presence in about 30 German universities, 3 Swiss universities and 5 to 6 Austrian ones.

We use a combination of different interviews: telephone interviewing to probe certain aspects of the CV, like language skills for example, and assessment centers and individual assessment to probe for critical behavior. Case interviewing is also used, but mainly for professionals, graduates and candidates with Ph.D.s. It is used primarily for Strategy and Change Management positions.

▶ **Do you feel applicants are becoming CV smarter?**

As far as I am concerned, no! Right now the market in Germany is pretty dry. On average a school leaver has two offers other than Andersen's when he graduates. AC does not select the candidates, the candidates select AC. They are all high potential people. This means they do not spend as much time as a good CV would require.

Too many of them are sloppy; they neglect showing the basic skills even when they are good. This comes from the fact that today they do not need to sell themselves. It is this kind of attitude which says: if they want me they will take me if not someone else will.

For us there are a certain number of 'musts.'

- An excellent academic record. In Germany this means 2 or less; in the US, a straight A record, and in France *Mention Très Bien*.

- Fluent English

- They must be motivated people who would like to be in the driver's seat. This means we would like to see this experience outside the purely academic field: organizing sports events, being a class spokesman, etc. Experience in a foreign country is also very useful.

On a bad CV important information will be missing: facts and dates do not correspond, a graduation does not correspond with the years of studies or with the date on the diploma. It will probably be too crowded, too messy. On the other hand, on a good CV facts, acts, diplomas, everything fits! The candidate will allow the recruiter to capture in two or three lines the idea that the applicant is motivated. He or she will show achievements, what they have done. They will use the right vocabulary: 'worked,' 'learned'...

In Germany, chronological CVs are the custom – we are used to reading it this way. If it is not chronological, there needs to be a logic guiding the recruiter: testimonies and facts. Diplomas from different countries, when they were earned in countries of 'Western Civilization' do not need to be translated. However, when an Australian says he went to California or Florida, to this or that institute, it is good to give us a hint on what was specific about this experience, what he wishes to highlight.

▶ How important is the letter ?

The letter is too often underrated. It does matter – if it's good! Different people with the same level of studies, graduating from the same school, have different personalities, different experience. In the letter, the recruiter expects to find out something new, personal, some experience and personal investments not mentioned before that make the person more interesting. The letter also makes it possible for us to check how well the candidate writes, even how good his or her spelling is. Too often, we are shocked to find our young consultants make a presentation in front of a client with spelling mistakes on the flipchart!

▶ Are electronic applications becoming more frequent?

Yes, they are getting more numerous. AC is publishing more Internet pages, where people can fill in their CV on-line. It allows the company to scan for the required criteria easier and faster and discard certain candidates right away, when they lack the critical skills.

To thine own self be true"[6]

In modern English this means "be truthful to yourself." Recruiters often point out that applicants should be very careful not to paint a portrait of themselves that clashes with what they are really like. The CV is absolutely crucial in landing the interview, and will most likely be re-read by the interviewer just before meeting the shortlisted applicant. If the CV has suggested a human dynamo 10 feet tall who naturally attracts people like a magnet, and the interviewee who walks through the door is slight, intellectual looking, and an attentive listener, the recruiter will go through the whole interview incredulous about what the applicant is saying.

In management, there is what is called the 'halo effect'. The 'halo effect' means that first impressions are difficult to overcome. Applicants instinctively realize this when they dress up for an interview, feeling that if they wore jeans, the recruiter would only remember the jeans and have trouble remembering the quality of their comments. It is the same with forged portraits; on the basis of your CV, recruiters form a kind of picture in their minds of the *kind* of person who will be sitting in front of them. If there is a great difference between the person in the CV and the person in front of them, there is the risk that they will believe neither.

If you think you have worth, then convey it as it is. It is very difficult to outperform a lie. One way to master the lying/telling the truth borderline, which is often a difficulty in sales language, is using a certain amount of *detail* about what you have done. Detail has a way of convincing people because they feel they are there, they can see the event you are describing. Sufficient detail about what you have done will make it unnecessary to use hype, overblown vocabulary or write sentences that are simply not true. This forms the subject of Chapter Four, but first let's take a look at the CV/Letter package and what it does.

---

6 Polonius to his son Laertes, in *Hamlet*, (I, iii), William Shakespeare.

Key points in chapter one

- Recruiters need you to write a good CV.

- Recruiters want to know what your skills are.

- Most of us hate writing a CV because it does not show what we really are.

- Most of us prefer to act than to write.

- To write a good CV you need to know the organizations well that you have worked with.

- To write a good CV you need to know yourself very well.

- Working hard on your CV will pay off.

- Always tell the truth.

- Les recruteurs s'attendent à recevoir un CV bien écrit.

- Tout recruteur cherchera à savoir quelles sont vos compétences

- Il n'est pas toujours facile d'écrire un CV car celui-ci ne fait pas ressortir ce que nous sommes vraiment !

- Beaucoup d'entre nous préfèrent agir plutôt qu'écrire.

- Il faut bien connaître les entreprises pour lesquelles vous avez travaillé afin d'écrire un bon CV.

- Il faut bien se connaître pour écrire un bon CV.

- N'hésitez pas à investir du temps dans la rédaction de votre CV, cela portera ses fruits.

- Ne mentez jamais.

What is the CV/Letter package?

When you put your CV into an envelope with your cover letter, it becomes a 'package' that represents you to recruiters, just like a salesman represents his company when he calls on customers. When we talk about the CV/Letter Package, we should start with the CV, since almost all job vacancy ads specify "Send CV" or "Send Resume." Although the letter plays an important role in the Package, it is better to start with the CV, for reasons we will see. So, let us start by defining the CV.

For years, we have started our seminars by asking our participants: "What is a CV?". Inevitably, we get answers that range from 'a history of my life' to 'a list of accomplishments.' Although the first is patently false, the second comes closer to the truth despite the unfortunate use of the word 'list'. We, on the other hand, tend to stress a CV's role as advertising. It reminds us of Norman Mailers' famous book, *Advertisements for Myself.*[1] Once we come to terms with the CV package being an advertisement for ourselves, it helps us a lot in planning what to say and how to say it. Then we will probably avoid writing what might look like history, because we will realize that buyers of products or services do not want to read history!

AN ADVERTISEMENT FOR YOURSELF

A CV package has a lot in common with advertising, and this means that good marketing analysis of the customer and his sensitivity to our communication is more relevant than drawing up a 'list' that we *think* he wants to read. Although content is the most important part

---

1 Mailer, N., *Advertisements for Myself,* Harvard University Press, 1992.

of the advertising, let's concentrate on the media itself for a minute to pick up some very important pointers on controlling your message.

Comparison with other forms of advertising

Limited time

Similarities with other advertising media need to be pointed out so that you can understand what is at stake. One thing you and your CV share with these media is the limited time you have to get your message across! Whether you are thinking of advertising – as some job seekers have done – on a billboard downtown or renting a truck to drive through the business center with your CV posted on the sides, exposure time is a key element in marketing your skills.

Such expensive advertisements might show how interested the applicant is in getting a job, but they do not necessarily show how interested the applicant is in getting a *certain* job. Attention-getting in no way replaces solid research on the company you are targeting; nor does it replace thinking about the link-up between your skills and the firm's needs. Nevertheless, these approaches do remind us of the need to fight for the reader's time. Companies spend huge sums on TV advertising, which is billed in terms of *seconds of exposure time* on the air, because it is so important to have time to drive the message home!

So, how much time will you typically get from a recruiter for your written CV/letter package? Although European hirers a decade ago asserted they devoted about 70 seconds to a CV/letter package to the Americans' 20 seconds, time has apparently taken its toll. Most European recruiters now also cite 20 seconds as the time they spend, on *average*, on the two crucial documents so painstakingly drafted by applicants seeking a job.

How much time will a recruter spend on your Letter and CV?

20 seconds!

All things taken into consideration, that's not so bad! Remember it is only an average. Therefore, your goal must be to get more than the average. It is obvious that a 'list' will not do that. If the reader does not find your advertising relevant to his needs, he will turn the page!

Limited media

Some will point out that, before he gets the interview, the job seeker only has the written word to help him, although he would like to use film and dialogue if he could. Chapter Four concentrates on the idea of making your CV into a kind of movie. Nevertheless, although some have used trucks, billboards and even balloons, except for sending a video, you will have to learn to use words. In the management of people, you will also have to use words!

A FIRST INTERVIEW

The CV – this advertisement for yourself – constitutes a kind of interview, an interview you are totally in control of. In this interview, you are replying to questions you feel the recruiter wants the answers to, but, to a large extent, it is you who are guiding the recruiter through a tour of the skills you want him to perceive. This is indeed the first interview, in what might become a series of interviews in the selection process. Recruiters stress that the CV is the only thing they have on which to base their decision to call an applicant to a face to face interview!

The CV: an interview to get an interview

The CV obviously deserves your utmost effort if, in essence, it is a first interview. Its purpose is usually to get you a next interview. Yet, it should be pointed out that very often, as in the case of looking for summer jobs or internships in foreign countries, the CV package is not written to get you the interview, but to get the job itself! For a two-month internship abroad, a recruiter will seldom ask you to come for a face-to-face interview: he will base his decision entirely on what he reads in your package. In this case, your CV is your only shot at it.

This 'make it or break it' approach often constitutes a rough hurdle for job-seekers and especially for university students, who are used to receiving marks for their university work, often on a highly gradated scale ranging from 1 to 20, sometimes from 0 to 100. Often they have piloted their way through university aiming at 'passing' courses that did not interest them much, often with a second exam session to allow them to make up a bad grade. Thus, they find it difficult to write a CV which will not be marked according to a university system which bends over backwards to recognize the differences between the excellent and the less excellent and more or less ensure all students a degree, if possible. Suddenly, they find themselves working on a kind of report of their activities for which there is no graduated scale of marking, and where they have to aim at total quality or possibly lose the battle. In CV-writing, there are only two marks: your application goes in the trash, or you receive a letter!

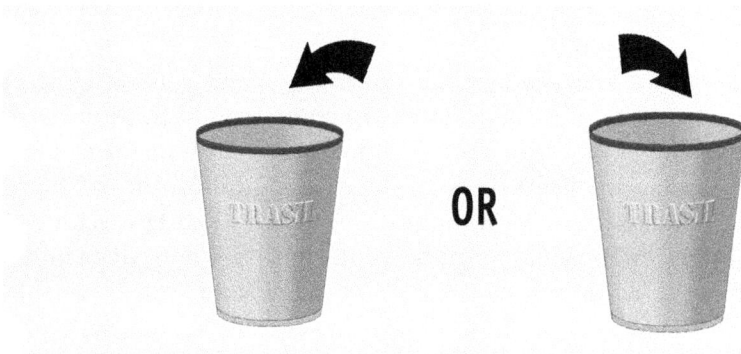

OR

How to understand the interviewer/ reader ?

What can we do to see into the reader's personality and value system? To continue our comparison between marketing logic and CV-writing, we might usefully fall back on the concept of the 'black box' in consumer marketing, which stresses how difficult it is to see into the buyer's decision-making process. This is important for writers who tend to put a lot of details in their CVs but do not analyze why they are putting them in, or what they are really communicating to the employer. This is particularly true in the realm of personal interests where the student often throws in a lot of information about what he or she likes to read, leisure activities and hobbies. Usually this 'catch-all' fails to perform any useful purpose, because the writer is talking to himself rather than thinking about the reader's interpretation.

This is complex and frustrating, because younger job applicants, for instance, will write that they like movie-going, reading, or sports and feel they are showing something about their personality. They may even specify the kind of movies or reading they like, or list some 6 or 7 sports they practice! The problem is the reader's black box. He or she may not understand what you are trying to get across when you mention you like to go to the movies, nor when you specify the kinds of books you read. And if 6 or 7 sports are listed, this might be interpreted as meaning you have no time to work!

One of our students in the past wrote that she had done 10 years of modern dance and held a black belt in Karate. This was simply listed at the bottom of the CV and not mentioned in the letter. What was the employer to make of it? There is certainly nothing wrong with it, and it was the truth. But what was she trying to sell? We facetiously asked if she was looking for a job as a body guard, a comment which she did not like. Upon further probing, we found that she was proud of these things, but did not know exactly why. We also felt she should be proud of these things, but that she needed to communicate the 'why' of that pride to the employer and link it up with benefits she was offering to the organization. In the end, we worked out together that these interests and her devotion to them had a lot to do with challenge-taking, perseverance and a taste for excellence. But she needed to make the link-up for the reader and show that she knew herself well.

What is the reader like ?

Trying to figure out what the reader of your CV is like might well be a thankless task. Is he or she fat or thin, tall or short, athletic or sedentary? Will he or she appreciate your love of stamp-collecting or horseback-riding? Racist or not racist, macho or womens-libber, there is very little you can do to figure it out, nor is it worthwhile. In most countries, legislation has set down guidelines for fair hiring and avenues for protecting your rights in cases of abuse.

Your best approach is to remain professional. When you talk professionally, you have a much better chance of striking a chord with the hirer. Then, you are leaving the realm of the black box of decision and moving into the field of business-to-business marketing. When you sell goods or services business-to-business, decision criteria are typically tough-minded and, with a little thought, easily perceivable to us all.

What is the recruiter looking for ?

Even in busines-to-business marketing, we need to understand what it is that the customer buys. Modern sales techniques have moved a long way from the days when we felt a customer bought a product. You have undoubtedly all been trained in techniques which stress that customers buy benefits, not products! Therefore, what you market must clearly be the 'benefit bundle' that appeals to your buyer. The difference between a product and a benefit is all the difference between a physical object with technological characteristics and the service that it can accomplish for us. A benefit is getting something done that we want done! If you like classical dance and karate, for example, and put that on your CV, this 'liking' is simply part of *your technological* characteristics unless you can relate it to some service you can deliver to the reader of your CV.

Hirers do not hire people in themselves, they hire problem-solvers, people who will get done for them what they haven't got the time to do themselves. So, above all, they are looking for *skills*, skills translatable into benefits! If they are interested in personality, it is because they are seeking a personality that will work well with their organization's culture and contribute to the hoped-for benefits. So if you think saying something about your personality is important, you are right – but you have to show the employer what you mean.

An offer of benefits for the hirer

We hope you have now realized that the CV/letter package should be an offer of service, an offer of benefits to the employer. If it is not that, and also clearly spelled out, there is no sense writing it. The hirer will be skimming through large numbers of CVs to shortlist a handful of applicants to interview, and he or she will select those who have made their offer of services and skills more clearly than the others. You are in control!

UNDERSTANDING THE TWO PARTS OF THE CV/LETTER PACKAGE

Everybody knows that what we call the CV package includes the CV itself and a cover letter. Yet there is often some confusion as to which does what! What are you supposed to put in the CV and what in the letter? Should the two documents include the same information? Should they use the same kind of style? Why even bother to write the letter at all?

The last question is not as silly as it might seem. Many of our seminar participants have pointed out that recruiters ask for CVs, but rarely letters. This means the CV is a must, but what about the letter? After all, a short letter saying "Please read my CV," might suffice! Many applicants write letters that are not much more than that. Even some recruiters say that applicants should not spend too much time on the letter. These recruiters say that they count much more on the CV in their selection process. We feel recruiters have come to say this because so few candidates write interesting letters, letters that provide them with a necessary complement of information to the CV.[2] Since they don't expect to get useful letters, they stress that at least the CV has got to be good!

The truth is quite different: you have two documents to make your case with. If both the letter and the CV are hard-hitting and contribute separately, yet jointly, to painting a portrait of a person who can do a job well for the company, it would be foolish not to invest your energy equally in both! In Chapter Seven we will show

---

2 See Interview with Margarida Faustino, Johnson & Johnson, Chapter 7, page 242.

you ways of writing that are a real addition to your CV, a letter that counts!

It should also be pointed out that in some countries, England and France for instance, some companies stress the need for a letter and specifically request it be handwritten. When they ask for handwritten letters, it is often simply because they want to see if you write legibly, or, they may submit the letters to graphology tests. You should, of course, comply with that request. The CV, on the other hand, should always be typed!

The further question of whether graphology, or handwriting analysis, has cross-border validity, is for specialists to decide. It is not at all sure that Germans write like the French or the English, thus in transnational applications the question of handwriting seems less important. What is sure, is that *content* is crucial, so let us deal with other reasons for writing *both* a CV and a letter. What does each of the documents do? We might sum up the specificity of each by saying this: the letter tells and the CV shows!

◄ THE CV PACKAGE ►

The Letter "tells" · The CV "shows"

What does the letter tell ?

A *good* letter can make a serious contribution to landing you an interview. It is the first thing the reader sees when he opens the envelope – which is why it is called the *cover letter* – even if it may not be the first thing he or she reads. A good letter does many useful things:

• First, it says "Hello"
• It tells them why you are writing
• It tells them what you know about the company and why you are applying to them
• It tells the company what benefits you offer
• It says what you want in return

Saying 'Hello'

This is a very important thing that a CV cannot do. You have to 'knock on the door' and introduce yourself. Reach out to shake hands! This first greeting sets the tone for the whole meeting you are having with the employer.

Telling them why you are writing

Put this right up front! A lot of applicants feel they should 'beat about the bush' as opposed to saying straight out why they are writing. They figure they have to get the reader's interest before mentioning what they want. This, of course, is the completely wrong way to go about getting anybody's interest. A job application is not a mystery novel! Nobody likes to read a whole letter and find out at the end why the sender wrote it. Typically, if we don't get the point, we put it aside and read something more interesting.

Tell the employer from the start that you are hoping to fill a certain position, applying for a summer job, or seeking an internship. This way there will be no misunderstanding. In the case of applying for an internship, for instance, if you write a whole letter full of impressive sales arguments and only tell the employer at the end that you are simply applying for an internship – when he thought you were seeking a full-time job – you may make him angry and spoil all your efforts. Being direct and 'to the point' can go a long way to advancing your cause. It can even help you land an internship where none existed – because you have convinced the employer that you can do a job he needs done. If not, it might provide you with a reference to an internship opportunity with another company he knows about.

Talking about your knowledge of the company

When we speak with recruiters, it is amazing how many companies mention that applicants send off a letter and CV to them without showing any knowledge of their business and current challenges. Sometimes, applicants even misspell the company's name! This flagrant lack of interest coupled with an overly effusive sales pitch can really put a hirer off! His or her first reaction will be to toss the CV in the trash.

On the other hand, when you show you know something of the company's recent history as well as its field of business and then make an effort to fit your background and skills in with its operating requirements, you are demonstrating that, at the very least, you care! The hirer is fully aware that you may not have always been totally fascinated by his company's field of activity, but he will appreciate your doing your homework – as he would expect of any executive in the firm.

Offering benefits

The modern application letter should make a clear offer of benefits to the recruiting company. It is only natural that the letter should follow the changes that have taken place in the CV. The old administrative style Curriculum Vitae in Europe – which was often just a 'list' – has given way to a more energetic, skills-oriented communication. The letter that accompanies it should offer services linked to the skills shown on this kind of CV! Recruiters are very outspoken about their desire to read letter/CV packages where applicants make such an offer.

When you write a letter that offers benefits or when you spell out your proposal of services, you are entering into the first phase of a work contract by showing awareness of the job description you are ready to fulfill. At the very least, by showing clearly the kind of person the company will be hiring, you are helping the recruiter leap ahead a couple of interviews. In doing this, you are shifting your application from the 'maybe' pile to the 'to be interviewed' pile.

Maybe...   **To be interviewed**

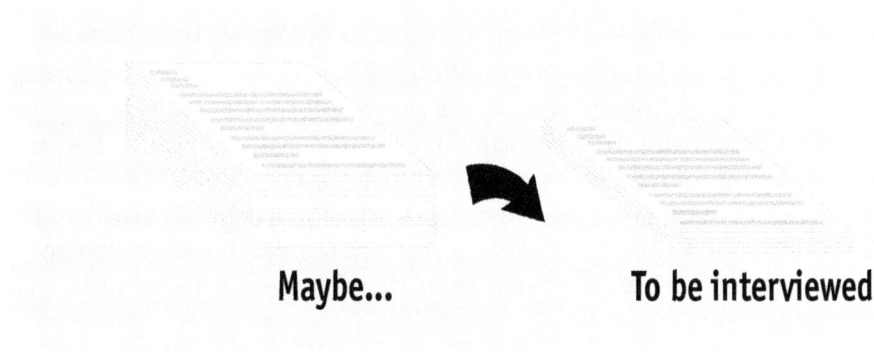

Saying what you want in return

To younger applicants – students and graduates – it might seem a bit bold to talk about what they hope to get out of the bargain, at this stage of the application. Even with older applicants, we are not suggesting that you mention salary or a company car in your first approach. What we are suggesting is that you be clear about opportunities you are seeking. For those of you who are applying for an internship, it may be learning and personal development. It is natural to say so. Above all, show that you are not coming in 'just for the ride,' but that you hope to take something away from your experience. People who want to get something for themselves out of their work are the kinds of learners who always have something to give as well! For those of you seeking a starting position with a company; you are looking for a career – with potential for growth! This too should be said, because it also offers commitment!

What does the CV show ?

If employers emphasize the importance of a CV for their recruiting process, it is because they hope you will write in a way that lets them see you *on the job*. Therefore, a CV is successful when

- It shows you working
- It shows the problems you have dealt with
- It shows your involvement
- It shows results you have reached
- It shows skills that will produce benefits

Showing yourself working

All of Chapter Four is devoted to teaching you how to turn your CV into a kind of 'movie' that allows the employer to 'zoom in on' the performance-oriented individual you are trying to show. For the time being, remember that the employer has never worked with you, and if, through your CV, you can provide him with a 'picture' of how you work and 'get things done', you stand a much better chance of being called for an interview than the CV writer who simply lists a series of jobs.

Showing problems you have dealt with

Include in your CV solid information about the kinds of problems you have dealt with in the past or are dealing with now. This will allow the employer to see your capabilities at work on problems that may be similar to those faced in his company. If you seek out information on the recruiting company's business and the job opening, you will be able to link up the kinds of problems you have solved with those the recruiter wants solved.

Showing your involvement

Involvement or commitment in a job is something that can never be communicated in a one-line description of a job or internship like the following 'flat' example from a 'list' CV:

No involvement!

| July-August 1999 | Marketing survey for X Company |

It is in the details that you provide when showing yourself working, solving problems and reaching results that will have the effect of conveying your commitment to your assignment. You will have to devote great care to working out these details for your CV, because they will automatically help you show your involvement!

Showing your results

The next chapter focuses in detail on the concepts of results and skills. It is crucial that *outcomes* you have achieved be spelled out in a CV. All firms need people that produce *outcomes*. If your CV does not clearly get across the results you have attained, the employer will get the impression that no personal growth has taken place, that you were just 'marking time'.

Showing skills you have that will produce benefits

You must learn to *show* skills. Skills are not easy qualities to communicate in general, nor even identify. Yet they are the essence of what we seek in an employee. A good CV must focus on accomplishments or outcomes in a way that makes the skills you used stand out! Then you can write a letter which talks about your skills explicitly, because they are supported by what is shown in the CV. This will allow you to make an offer of benefits you can produce for your future firm.

Interview # 3 :
AT CAP GEMINI, APPLICANTS SHOULD BE ABLE TO GET OUR INTEREST !

Interview with Carolyn Nimmy, Global Staffing Director, Cap Gemini, Barcelona, Spain.

Carolyn Nimmy is the Global Staffing Director for the Cap Gemini Group. Her role is to support the business as it globalizes by addressing HR and staffing challenges that need international solutions rather than geographic ones. Key projects have focussed on recruitment—developing the Cap Gemini Employer Brand, Internet recruiting, key role development, career development and facilitating better international movements of staff. She has also been involved in the Career Innovations Research Group—8 multinational companies who have come together to research Careers in the 21st Century.

▶ What do you look for in an applicant's CV?

The resume is an intricate part of the interview, as it is the initial 'opening' of the conversation you have with the applicant and therefore very important. The interview process will go into the CV in depth and probe much further the candidate's history and experience. The CV must be a concise synopsis of what candidates have done in the past and why they want to work for us. The way in which the individual interacts with us enables us to see how they will be able to interact with our clients – a key skill in our business. When we give information to our clients about a consultants skills, there are two parts:

- First a high-level profile for the client – this is the key selling document to arouse interest

- Second, there is a detail document that goes into more depth as to projects undertaken, business knowledge, key skills and competencies, etc.

Applicants should have this same business-like approach – capture our attention and then provide more detailed back-up information. Some applicants can be very frustrating because they ramble on, not sure themselves of where they are going or what they are looking to do. These people are not hired! We look for people with skills suited for certain industries and also for people with relevant technical skills. To work in our industry – consulting and IT services – we need people who are open minded, committed to life-long learning and flexible. Interpersonal and communication skills are essential to developing and maintaining client relationships. In this 'knowledge revolution' era for many employers, it is these 'soft' skills that are becoming increasingly important.

▶ How should candidates show they are able to work internationally?

Many applicants do not understand some of the basic requirements or challenges to be able to work internationally – understanding what it really means – not only in terms of languages, which are an essential basic requirement, but also to be able to show they have a global 'mindset' and that they can work and interact with many different cultures and nationalities. They must not be naïve about what working internationally really entails. Within Europe we perceive it to be very easy to work in the different EU countries – however, applicants in most cases need to be fluent in the language of the new country they wish to work in – our customers expect this of our consultants. Then there are other challenges that they must consider: where will my 'main' home be, my bank account, where will my kids go to school, where will my pension be and what about social security?, etc. We may have a European Economic Community, and the Euro is helping to give transparency on costs and pricing in some countries, but our employment environments are very different and candidates need to understand this.

▶ How do you expect the CV to be structured?

We do not demand the CV to be in a particular format. The CV needs to be concise and include some personal details relating to country and languages. Above all, applicant need to be able to express clearly what they are offering – capabilities, skills, knowledge and expertise. We do prefer to see what the individual has done most recently first and then work backwards from there, but we do not need to see everything they have ever done! The most important information must be 'upfront'.

▶ What is the importance of the cover letter?

The worst thing is a 'phony' letter with too much exaggeration on what a great company they think we are. A straightforward statement from the heart is so much more believable. Nowadays most of our applications are coming through the Web, so a simple truthful statement like, for example: "I have read your pages on the web and I feel I can work here because....., I have done .....I can do this for you ...... ". This gives us a much better idea and clearer information. Attaching a profile that is a more factual document and backs up what you are looking to do is a combination with the cover letter.

▶ You mentioned the Web. Has Internet changed the way hiring is being done?

Yes, I think new trends are being set. More young people are contacting us directly via the web. There is a real revolution going on here with people spontaneously applying – or even just starting up an 'electronic conversation' that leads to them sending in their profile. What We do look out for, however, is the job-hopper people who change jobs every few months – this is not what we are looking to see in a CV – we like to see some loyalty.

I have been surprised by how some senior people working for our competitors will approach us through the Web where in the past they would have been unlikely to send us their resume through the mail/post. We may get more applicants through the Web than some other companies because we are an IT company. However, whichever way a candidate applies, the most important thing is to really show what you are capable of in a clear and concise manner!

Key points in chapter two

- A CV is an advertisement for yourself.

- You have about 20 seconds to communicate your skills.

- The CV is an interview to get another interview.

- You have to understand how the recruiter thinks.

- The CV and the Letter have to work together.

- The Letter tells the recruiter what you know and what you have to offer.

- The CV shows how you work and what you can do because you have done it.

- Un CV est une publicité pour vous-même.

- Vous avez environ 20 secondes pour montrer vos compétences.

- Le CV est un premier entretien d'embauche qui doit vous mener à l'entretien suivant.

- Vous devez obligatoirement comprendre la manière de penser d'un recruteur.

- Le CV et la lettre doivent être un véritable tandem.

- Dans la lettre vous expliquerez ce que vous savez faire et ce que vous avez à offrir.

- Dans le CV vous montrerez votre façon de travailler et ce que vous savez faire puisque vous l'avez déjà fait.

Preparing to write

As you read through this chapter, remember that your goal is to be able to communicate in terms clear to an employer that:

1. you understand a great deal about what is needed for the job, and
2. that you know your skills well enough to be sure you can fill it.

FIND OUT ABOUT THE JOB

Most likely, if you are reading this book, you have been studying economics, business, management, sciences or engineering for several years or intend to do so. You may be a professional who wants to change careers. In any case, you are aware of the business community, the world of companies. Either your studies in university or business school or some years of work experience have sensitized you to the functions that characterize a profession in marketing, finance, production, general management, and so on. That means you have a pretty good idea about what kinds of activities are carried out in any department, even if you have never worked in the one in which you are applying for a job or internship.

Read about the profession

Textbooks abound on every possible profession in business; these books provide full courses on how to perform the activities basic to work in the field that interests you. The specialized press carries reports on companies as well as interviews with operatives from all functional fields and industries. If you are a student, your own university marketing, production and finance departments have sources you can consult, and, of course, the faculty can brief you on what kinds of work are done and what you will be expected to do, in their own fields of specialization in any company.

You need to know about all these sources of information, because often you are applying to work in a field or industry you have never worked in before. This is very frequent, since all of us, at one time in our lives, have never worked before, or have to change professions. Another case is where you have worked in a field, for instance accounting, but have never carried out financial analysis, even though your educational background has prepared you for it. In that case, remember that universities often hold job forums where you can pick up a lot of information about what jobs specifically require. At these forums you can learn what it is like to work in a certain department or on a certain project.

Study job descriptions

Your best possible guide to understanding what a job requires is to study the job description. In many instances, you may consult fairly detailed descriptions of a very wide range of positions in all fields right in your own campus library or placement service. These job descriptions explain what responsibilities a position entails and what skills are needed. They will also often tell you what the future will be like for this profession. Many books are on the market providing a long lists of careers and including typical jobs in each field, with information on the educational background needed, current salary ranges, typical assignments, career outlook and often the desirable skills and personal qualities. In the box on the opposite page, you will find a typical job description that might be published in many sources. Study it for a minute.

You can see that job descriptions are very valuable tools. First, they help you decide what kind of job you want to do. Second, they assist you in understanding what kinds of skills are needed for the position.

Recruitment officer

Responsibilities
- Implements the recruitment policy established by the Human Resource Manager
- Selects applicants for managerial positions, alone or working with a recruiting agency
- Defines profile requirements and drafts press advertisements
- Handles the selection process for all internal or external recruitment, including testing and interviewing
- Manages transfers, dismissals and resignations
- Coordinates relations with professional schools and universities

Skills required
- Designing interviews to ascertain applicants' 'fit' and long-term growth potential in line with company objectives
- Insightful interviewing to sound out potential problems
- Building relationships with placement officers and academic officials
- Interfacing diplomatically with departmental heads

Education
Same profile as for the Human Resource Manager. Usually a degree from a business school or a post-graduate specialization in Human Resources or Personnel Management.

Outlook for the profession
In recent years, companies have turned to recruiting agencies to perform these tasks. Thus the function is often outsourced and the internal recruiting officer transferred to other duties in Human Resources.

One warning, however: not all job descriptions spell out the skills needed in a way that you can relate to. You will have to audit your own background and skills to find where you can match the requirements of the job. In the example of the Recruitment Officer in the box, for example, the verbs in the *Skills Required* section might be separated out from the rest of the sentence. This would leave:

- designing interviews

- insightful interviewing

- sounding out potential problems

- building relationships

- interfacing diplomatically

Taken out of a direct relation with recruiting experience, you might find that you had many of these skills – skills developed through other experience – and which you might well carry over into a new job, such as the one given in the example. On your voyage of self discovery, it would be far more useful to determine whether you are good at designing interviews and building relationships than focusing on your knowledge of, or training in, recruiting itself. Skills have a way of being useful in many different situations. In this case, if the applicant reviewed his skills apart from the recruiting context, he might well be able to sit for an interview for a similar job and draw attention to his skills along *generic* lines rather than 'job-specifically'. In reading the *Outlook for the profession* at the bottom of the description, he might realize as well that there is an opportunity for his talents with recruiting agencies.

Generic skills are skills that might be used in a variety of situations and which are not linked to a specific functional position, although they may have been developed in a particular job. "Drawing up market survey polls" is a job-specific skill. It is directly linked to marketing. On the other hand, "working out interviews that provide solid, easy-to-process information" is a *generic* skill. It could be applied in a variety of information – gathering situations – taking censuses for the government, recruiting, running periodic personal evaluation interviews, etc.

As you go through this book, you will find out that generic skills can be very important when you are starting or changing your career!

FIND OUT ABOUT THE COMPANY

Too many applicants overlook the need to find out about the company. They need to do their homework like good students! Perhaps they have a feeling they are going to work in a department, not in a company; that they are going to concentrate on marketing a product, and, to do that, they do not need too much information about the company. Perhaps some applicants feel they will learn about the company during the interview or will have enough time to read up about it on the train – on their way to the interview!

We have found it very difficult to ascertain just why so many of our seminar participants had not done their homework on the target company before writing their CV. Above all, we believe that they were just working so hard on doing research on themselves – to get their CVs ready – that they didn't find the time to do research on the company!

It was very important that the person interviewed had already put himself or herself 'into our shoes' before the interview and knew the skills we were looking for, was sensitive enough to understand what we needed. In the end, the successful candidate knew what benefits to sell. The person we hired knew he would have to train other people. He explained he liked to teach, he had done some teaching in the past and was proud of it, had really enjoyed it. That's what I mean by selling benefits!
Margarida Faustino, Johnson & Johnson

Employers, on the other hand, are often shocked by applications from candidates who, in their letter, make no reference to their industry and show little awareness of the recent developments in it. All the self-knowledge in the world cannot make up for an apparent lack of interest in the firm where you are going to apply your skills.

Find out all you can about a company, its officers and its recent decisions. You must brief yourself fully on a potential employer just as a sales person briefs himself about a prospective customer. Just as your knowledge of the potential customer will assist you in addressing problems that interest him, in putting yourself 'on the same wave-length', knowing about your future employer's interests and problems will allow you to design your CV in a way related to those interests and problems, and really talk *to him* in your letter. What makes the difference between a personal and a circular letter is not merely the use of the person's name, but also talking about things that are of mutual interest.[1]

Sources of information are plentiful for most companies: the library, magazines, Internet, but the company itself is the richest source of all. Get in touch with your target company through its Internet site, e-mail it a request for information, or just pick up the phone and call! Both Internet and calling may serve a double purpose: first, you can request company literature – the annual report is by far the most informative about strategy, recent changes and future plans – and, second, you can get the name of a person to write to! We will take this up again in Chapter Seven. For now, just remember that a letter addressed to a *name* is far more powerful than one addressed to a position – such as Marketing Manager.

FIND OUT ABOUT YOURSELF

Research into yourself is the most important research you will ever do! In Chapter One, we pointed out the very great importance that knowing how to write a CV can have for your career, because of what you learn to do during the *thinking* and the *writing*. We also pointed out that a CV is an 'offering of skills to solve a company's problems'. Now, in this phase of your preparation, you are going to start making an inventory of your skills and understanding how to relate those to career opportunities. In doing so, you will also be developing your communications skills – all the better to communicate your *worth*.

Think in terms of Sales

As pointed out a couple of paragraphs above, you must go about preparing a CV as you might work out a sales talk to a prospective customer. Modern marketing techniques focus on the delivery of

---

1 See interview with Margarida Faustino, Johnson & Johnson, Chapter 7, page 242.

benefits, and 'benefit bundles' to buyers, not products! Benefit segmentation is a way of dividing up buyer groups according to the benefits they seek from a product or service, rather than on the basis of the product itself. Employers most often think in terms of 'deliverables'[2], which may be defined simply as benefits you can deliver: something you can do that they want done!

What is it they want done?

We have talked a lot about industry and company knowledge. For CV-writing this might more accurately be expressed as 'customer knowledge'. Figuring out what the employer/customer wants done is relatively easy if you follow the steps listed at the beginning of this chapter. Then, in movie-making terms, you are going to have to use your script-writing ability to 'picture' what you will be doing exactly if you land the job you are applying for. This 'picturing' capability runs through this book and is carefully developed in Chapter Four, which deals with showing yourself *performing* in your various accomplishment areas.

What is it you can do?

Now for the hardest part: active people tend to charge ahead, although intelligently, and often take little time to stand back and look at themselves. Looking at oneself often seems to belong more to the introspective, inwardly-turned artist-type person. Yet, knowing oneself is key in getting ahead in the world of management, so obviously it is not reserved to a group of people who 'watch the world go by'. Interviewers, just like the MBA screening committees dealt with in Chapter Eight, will want you to know yourself so that you can tell them what they need to know. They don't want to have to 'pull it out of you'; they want it on a platter!

As in sales, the customer does not want to have to ask you a lot of questions about all the characteristics of your product – in this case, yourself – but expects you to relate your characteristics directly and immediately to his needs. You are expected to have done your homework on your own skills set, as you are expected to have done your homework on the company's needs.

---

2 See Interview with Valerie Robert, *Procter and Gamble*, Chapter 4, page 112.

Knowing what you can do!

You abilities and your personality traits form a package that might be likened to the performance and features of a product. Complete 'product knowledge' is essential to a good salesman, not because he or she will talk about all of them, but because it makes it possible to link up 'what can be done' to 'what needs to be done.' This is the same as 'what you can do' and what the company 'needs you to do'. If you have this knowledge about yourself and about the company, you will then be able to sell benefits.

What are skills

Skills are typically expressed as gerunds, or, in other words, they finish in 'ing.' The reason for this is obvious in English: we are good at doing something. This *doing, speaking, convincing, getting along with people,* etc. is also the tense in English which 'shoots' movies. You will find in the long list of sample skills on the following pages that they are almost all in 'ing', because we want you to 'picture' yourself doing those things.

Skills develop as a natural part *of living* and *doing,* and you don't even need to have worked before to be able to offer these skills to an employer. Undoubtedly, it is better to have some kind of work experience when applying for a job, and often, experience in a similar field. But we all have to get our first job sometime and, to do so, convince an employer that we have skills to offer. Writing a CV if you have never worked is, of course, a major challenge, and, in almost every seminar we have ever run there is at least one participant who has not yet had what could be called a 'job'. Our challenge is getting such participants to talk about what they have done that they are 'proud of', because it is in describing what they did that the skills they used will come to the foreground, even if it was not during a 'job'.

Indeed, it is through activity that we discover, develop and *sharpen* our skills. There are three major sources of skills development:

• Abilities you have developed through *living*
• Abilities you have developed through *working*
• Abilities you have developed through *studying*

Abilities developed through living

Sports, clubs, charity activities, church activities, traveling, scouts, hobbies, building, painting, writing are all the kinds of activities that allow people to use their skills and perfect them. The list could go on, but the main thing to remember is that we have all *worked* on some project that got us involved and called on our skills. You must probe through your own background for these skills-developing occasions, whether your are among those who have had a job before or not, since many of these occasions may have allowed you to develop skills that are different, even richer, than those developed in so-called 'professional' situations.

Abilities developed through working

On-the-job-developed skills are perfect for writing a CV, of course. Then why is it so few applicants understand what skills were used or developed on the job, and so few communicate them well? We feel it has a lot to do with not understanding what skills are and not being used to talking about them! Almost all societies encourage their members not to *brag*. Ironically, however, success is often based on knowing "how to blow one's own horn" just enough![3] If you have concentrated on *doing* more than *talking* about it, you will find *talking* difficult. For you we have provided a list of general performance skills on the following pages. We hope the list will help you find your own skills in situations where you can recognize yourself. Remember that applicants typically feel that the job-linked skills they talk about should be technical in nature, like working on spreadsheets, carrying out financial analysis, performing market research, etc. Actually, much of what employers are looking for has to do more with human relations and problem-solving skills. These may be transferable from an entirely different business than their own, or from a function far-removed from what you are applying for. Thus, 'labeling' your skill correctly is very important when, later, you are selling the benefit it can produce in a new field of activity!

---

3 Blanchard, K. *The One Minute Manager.*
Also available in French: *Le Manager minute*, Éditions d'Organisation, 1987.

Abilities developed through studying

Most street-smart applicants will draw on their studies to emphasize fields of competence – and they are quite right to do so. What better chance for a person with no financial job experience, for instance, to point out that he or she has acquired a skill in financial analysis through his course work at the university. On the other hand, the very process of surviving at the university develops a variety of skills that should be stressed. These are skills like carrying out documentary research, synthesizing data, structuring reports, working with teams on projects, and so on. Many of these are more relevant to employers' needs – what they call project management skills – than the acquisition of specific technical skills in disciplinary fields.

A university education has become a must, not so much for the specific area knowledge or technical skills you may acquire, but because of more general skills like numeracy, literacy, and maturity skills that are developed – like focusing on results. What counts is the habit of working on projects, dealing with complex ideas, and working with people! You must search your own educational experience for the development of these kinds of skills.

In some countries, France for example, students are admitted to business schools on the basis of competitive examination. Students will have done two years of preparatory school after secondary school graduation or have a university degree before sitting the exam. The kinds of qualities that are tested for are: general literacy, mathematical reasoning capability and analytical and writing skills. Recruiters in France often say that, in itself, admission to a French business school is a guarantee that the applicant has acquired a good level of general education. This example should remind you of the value of skills developed outside the job market.

Skills and personality traits, the link

We all have trouble separating what we 'are' from what we 'do'. When we ask someone what another person is like, do they answer "Mike is helpful," or, "Mike helps out?" One answer uses an adjective and the other answer uses a verb. The main thing is we can say Mike is helpful because he has often helped out. His personality is proved because of the actions he has taken in the past!

When you start taking inventory of your 'self,' on your quest for self-knowledge, you will have to find examples of things you have done to prove to others (and to yourself) that you are what you say you are. Remember that if you say you are a *helpful* person to someone who doesn't know you, he may think you are bragging![4] If he is uninterested, he will say "really..." On the other hand, the interested stranger, or the skeptic – perhaps a recruiter – may well say, "really? give me an example." Once you have given an example, or several, of your 'helpfulness', you are on your way to saying, in essence, that it is a skill you have; that you are good at 'helping.' So you will have to prepare these examples in advance.

Now you realize that there is a strong link between the kind of person you 'are', and the services or benefits that come from the skills you are offering a potential employer! It is no surprise to say that a person is a whole! This is why employers say "I want this kind of person." It is because he sees the 'doer,' the person who will – by his nature – act to produce benefits with his skills for the firm. The main challenge for you, the CV writer, is in understanding it well enough to communicate it well.

You will need to draw up a list of character traits or qualities that adequately portray you as you feel you really are. Be ready to buttress this list with solid examples of your behavior that make the listener listen! On page 68, we have provided a list of common adjectives that might help you describe what kind of person you are. We suggest you go through the list and check off those that you feel apply to you. You must avoid checking off too many adjectives; select only those which define something important about you, that you consider fairly essential to your identity. No list is complete to describe the range of people, so we have left space in the box below for you to add other adjectives you feel apply to you. Later, in writing, you will only pull a few of all these adjectives out of inventory to say something major about yourself that offers a benefit to the employer.

---

4 See interview with Veli-Pekka Niitamo, *Nokia*, Chapter 6, page 209.

Adjectives to describe what kind
of person you are (see page 266 for translation into french)

Able to take stress	_____	Honest	_____
Aggressive	_____	Humorous	_____
Analytic	_____	Imaginative	_____
Assertive	_____	Insightful	_____
Capable	_____	Intellectual	_____
Careful	_____	Intelligent	_____
Cautious	_____	Natural	_____
Cheerful	_____	Observant	_____
Considerate	_____	Organized	_____
Creative	_____	Patient	_____
Curious	_____	Performance-oriented	_____
Dedicated	_____	Persistent	_____
Demanding	_____	Persuasive	_____
Dependable	_____	Practical	_____
Determined	_____	Precise	_____
Diligent	_____	Ready and willing	_____
Easy-going	_____	Resourceful	_____
Effective	_____	Responsible	_____
Efficient	_____	Risk-taking	_____
Energetic	_____	Self-confident	_____
Enterprising	_____	Self-starting	_____
Fast	_____	Sensitive	_____
Flexible	_____	Sincere	_____
Friendly	_____	Straightforward	_____
Goal-oriented	_____	Street-smart	_____
Go-getting	_____	Supportive	_____
Hard-working	_____	Thorough	_____
Helpful	_____	Thoughtful	_____
		Warm	_____

Now add any adjectives that are missing in the list

_____   _____   _____

_____   _____   _____

Kinds of skills

Skills overlap so much and have so many different applications, that they are difficult to classify. Nevertheless, we are going to point out three different conceptions of skills that might help you go about visualizing your own.

From the management science point of view

Traditionally, in management science courses at the university, you have learned that there are three basic kinds of skills in management: technical, human relations and conceptual. This is a useful categorization to help you understand what kinds of skills you have. Research has determined that your level in the chain of command has much to do with which kinds of skills you use the most, as the diagram on the next page shows.

Technical skills are those closest to the actual production of goods and services. This means knowing how to machine parts, keep books, and write up marketing questionnaires. These are skills used most by operatives. First-line managers will need these the most, as they oversee the work of the operatives and should themselves be technical specialists, giving advice and correcting. They may have themselves been promoted from the technical ranks. As managers move up in the hierarchy, they will typically use this specialized knowledge of operations less, and use more conceptual skills.

Conceptual skills have a great deal to do with systems logic. They are the more abstract thinking skills which enable managers to see the organization as a whole, to see the relationships between the various parts of the organization, and to visualize how the firm fits into its larger environment. Although all managers need conceptual skills, they are particularly important to top-level managers and needed for strategic thinking. In the last two decades, Total Quality Management and Japanese management techniques have pointed out the need to develop these kinds of skills among workers so that they can take more responsibility for the operation as a whole: *they develop worker managers!*

Human relations skills are needed at every level of management. If management is not "doing" but "getting things done through others," it is logical for human skills to be important at every level. Human skills include communicating, motivating, and leading. Above all, managers ensure information flows; therefore communication with others is at the center of their profession, gathering and disseminating information so that the organization functions.

The 3 Basic Kinds of Skills and their Relative Importance for different levels of Management

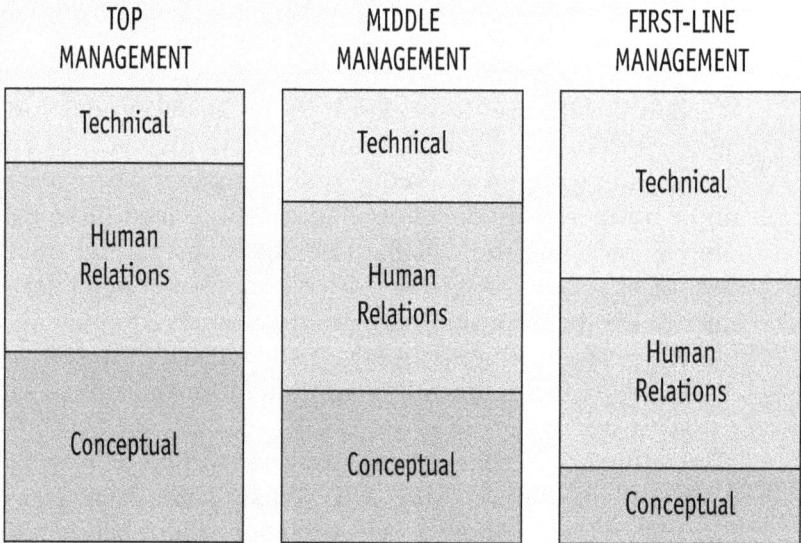

TOP MANAGEMENT	MIDDLE MANAGEMENT	FIRST-LINE MANAGEMENT
Technical	Technical	Technical
Human Relations	Human Relations	Human Relations
Conceptual	Conceptual	Conceptual

Ironically enough, recent graduates aiming at management careers feel they will be hired for their technical skills, which, fresh out of school, is what they typically lack the most. Although they will receive some 'technical training' in university and during their internships, their education will develop mostly conceptual skills, like those used by top management – or multi-faceted workers! When you study business and management in the university, you are educated to take a broad view of the organization, the kind developed in classes on corporate strategy. Your human relations skills will come from whatever occasions you have had to interface on projects with other people – at school, in outside activities, or on the job. And these skills will be among the most important for you to realize – and communicate!

From the company point of view

Employers will probably not use the same vocabulary as professors of management science, although their conclusions will be the same. They are more likely to scrutinize job candidates for two kinds of skills: *technical skills* – what might be termed 'job specific' skills – *and general performance skills*. They often refer to these as 'hard' skills and 'soft' skills.

Job-specific skills are best developed during summer jobs, internships, specialized training courses, or in practicing a profession. These kinds of experience can easily be pointed out on a CV and linked to the job you are applying for, if the experience is relevant, job-wise. On the other hand, general performance skills have a lot more to do with human relations and project management skills. They fall more into the category of 'working well with people', 'getting things done' and 'taking responsibility'. Too often, applicants overlook the importance of these 'soft' skills. You must learn to sell these to a recruiter just as clearly as you do technical skills.

Below you will find a chart which shows the findings of research carried out in the US about the skills most valued by American employers from recent university graduates. It clearly shows the stress on performance skills.

Employers' ranking of skills of entry-level applicants

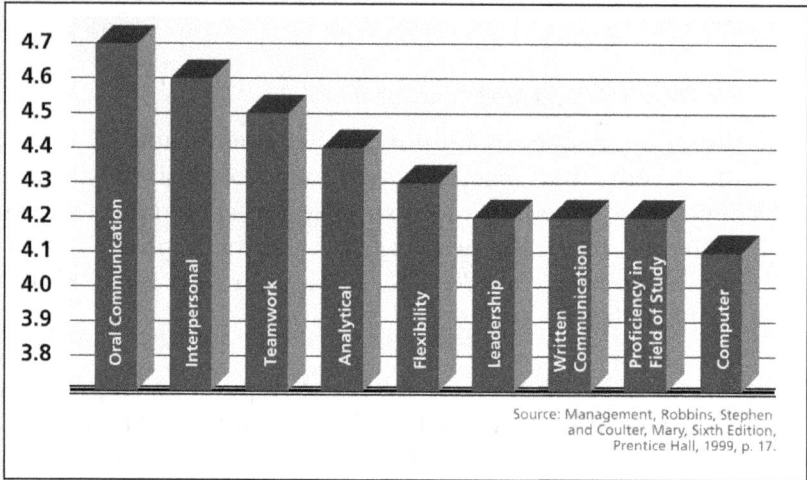

Skill	Value
Oral Communication	4.7
Interpersonal	4.6
Teamwork	4.5
Analytical	4.4
Flexibility	4.3
Leadership	4.2
Written Communication	4.2
Proficiency in Field of Study	4.2
Computer	4.1

Source: Management, Robbins, Stephen and Coulter, Mary, Sixth Edition, Prentice Hall, 1999, p. 17.

Now analyze your skills

Now, it is time to sit down and analyze your own skills. Take a complete skills inventory. On the following pages, we have drawn up a long list of general performance skills to help you in your inventory-taking. We feel you probably know your own technical skills well. The generic skills we have listed are organized by situations. *You should try to shoot a 'movie' of yourself in similar situations as you read through the list to determine what you are particularly good at.* Place a tick in the box next to any skill that you believe you have; do you see yourself in this scene of the 'movie?' Later you can go back over the skills you have ticked off and take the most important ones and develop them in the Skill Discovery Boxes that follow the list.

THINKING SITUATIONALLY
TRY TO SEE YOURSELF WHEN YOU ARE:

ON THE PHONE

DOING:	AM I GOOD AT?:	

**Responding on
the phone**

Communicating warmth ☐
Listening intently ☐
Picking up essential information ☐
Getting down the facts ☐
Following up the problem ☐
Creating an image of helpfulness ☐

Initiating on the phone

Getting through to the person I want ☐
Managing to get the information I want ☐
Settling on a date, ensuring follow-up action ☐
Expediting matters over the phone ☐
Leaving the person on the other end with
    a good feeling at the end ☐

INTERFACING WITH OTHERS

DOING:	AM I GOOD AT?:	

**Interfacing with
suppliers/customers**

Communicating warmth ☐
Remembering people's names ☐
Sensing people's feelings, reactions, and attitudes ☐

Interfacing with coworkers

Remembering coworkers' names ☐
Treating people fairly ☐
Showing patience with difficult or demanding people ☐
Being sensitive to people's feelings, reactions,
    and attitudes ☐
Knowing the strengths and weaknesses of people ☐
Being thought of as highly reliable,
    'somebody you can count on' ☐

As a subordinate

Assisting superiors in making decisions ❑
Supporting my boss
Getting people at all levels to support and
    carry through decisions which have come
    down from the top ❑
Gaining trust and respect of key people ❑
Making effective recommendations ❑
Respecting policies and procedures ❑
Being perceived as trustworthy, honest ❑

Persuading

Influencing others' ideas ❑
Being a good go-between among groups ❑
Helping reach consensus among diverse groups ❑
Gaining support from those affected by decisions ❑
Getting people to change their views
on long-held beliefs ❑
Getting coworkers and customers to reveal their needs ❑
Really listening to people and sensing their true needs ❑

AT MEETINGS

DOING:	AM I GOOD AT?:

Planning for meetings

Setting goals to be reached ❑
Drawing up a clear agenda ❑
Getting people to come prepared to the meeting ❑
Timing the meeting well ❑

Running meetings

Holding useful meetings ❑
Using supports well/ Using audiovisual aids ❑
Controlling interventions ❑
Getting participation from everybody ❑
Maintaining productive group discussions ❑

Participating at meetings

Listening intently ❑
Open to other people's ideas ❑
Taking the floor assertively ❑
Respecting the organizational meeting style
    (assertive or non-assertive) ❑

Making suggestions effectively ❑
Building on others' ideas ❑
Originating ideas ❑
Suggesting courses of action ❑
Getting to the heart of a problem ❑

ON THE TEAM

DOING: **AM I GOOD AT?:**

Fitting in with the team and the culture

Playing as a team member ❑
Being responsive to people's feelings and needs ❑
Acting tactfully ❑
Building rapport ❑
Feeling comfortable with all kinds of people ❑
Accepting responsibility for mistakes ❑
Accepting other people's ideas ❑
Giving credit to others ❑
Giving thanks for help ❑

Sensing when it's good to compromise
    and when it's good to fight ❑
Working smoothly with others ❑
Gaining people's confidence in my actions ❑
Improvising under stress ❑
Working solutions out with a group ❑
Handling difficult people ❑
Getting a feel for the group culture ❑

Standing out

Taking the initiative when opportunity appears ❑
Taking over ❑
Motivating/Inspiring people ❑
Getting elected/Getting selected as a group leader ❑
Helping bring about change ❑
Activating sluggish groups ❑
Settling disagreements ❑
Overcoming blockages ❑
Calming down conflict situations ❑
Winning people's cooperation ❑

HEADING THE TEAM

DOING:	AM I GOOD AT?:

Training the members

Assisting people in making decisions ❏
Encouraging others to take charge ❏
Answering questions clearly ❏
Explaining difficult ideas and concepts ❏
Teaching and training ❏
Developing training materials that help
    and speed up learning ❏
Keeping classes interesting ❏
Presenting interesting lectures ❏

Leading the members

Developing a team that works together well ❏
Making people belong to the group ❏
Knowing when to delegate ❏
Increasing morale ❏
Mediating in conflict situations ❏
Gaining support to carry through projects ❏
Getting others to share my vision of things ❏
Being recognized as the leader for the situation ❏
Integrating the team's ideas ❏
Giving recognition to the members ❏

**Communicating
with the members**

Sensing when people aren't understanding ❏
Being able to reword assignments
    and communication so people understand ❏

SOLVING PROBLEMS

DOING:	AM I GOOD AT?:

**Tackling/coping
with problems**

Anticipating problems ❏
Solving problems ❏
Straightening out messes ❏
Bringing order out of a chaotic situation ❏
Determining fundamental causes of problems ❏

Analyzing problem drivers

Interpreting/Evaluating data and reports ❑
Analyzing trends ❑
Designing methods for collecting
    or analyzing information ❑
Simplifying complex ideas ❑
Spotting non-logical thinking ❑
Seeing both sides of an issue ❑
Synthesizing ideas ❑
Diagnosing problems ❑
Constantly looking for a better way ❑
Identifying more efficient ways of doing things ❑
Summarizing findings ❑

General project skills

Finding and obtaining the resources
    necessary for a task ❑
Implementing new programs ❑
Managing projects ❑
Organizing projects and programs ❑

Carrying out research

Following up on leads ❑
Investigating ❑
Organizing large amounts of data and information ❑
Researching in a library ❑
Sifting important information from unimportant ❑
Tracking down information ❑
Building a good knowledge base ❑
Developing new testing methods ❑
Getting people to provide information ❑
Producing surveys or questionnaires ❑
Perceiving relationships between things ❑
Detecting cause and effect relationships ❑
Using statistical data ❑
Developing working hypotheses ❑

Deciding

Making difficult decisions ❑
Acting decisively in crisis situations ❑
Making up my mind fast ❑
Stepping in and controlling an emergency ❑
Recognizing the need for change and being
    willing to undertake it ❑

Spotting 'windows of opportunity' ☐
Finding new ways of doing things ☐
Seeing the value in older ways of doing things ☐
Calling into question my first approach
    in favor of a better one ☐
Acting fast to keep small problems
    from becoming big problems ☐
Avoiding jumping to conclusions ☐
Weighing the pros and cons of an issue ☐

ON YOUR OWN

DOING: AM I GOOD AT?:

Conceiving

Imagineering/Conceiving and generating ideas ☐
Improvising ☐
Innovating ☐
Conceptualizing/ Seeing the big picture ☐
Building on others' ideas ☐
Synthesizing ideas from a group
    and turning them into a plan for action ☐

Designing

Seeing things others don't see ☐
Bringing together two distinct concepts
    to produce something original ☐
Conceiving visual representations
    of ideas and concepts ☐
Sensing what people will understand ☐
Envisioning the finished product/sensing
    how it will all come together ☐

Planning

Prioritizing ☐
Anticipating problems and people's reactions ☐
Planning programs or projects ☐
Setting attainable goals ☐
Scheduling effectively ☐
Managing my time ☐
Accurately predicting results of proposed action ☐
Accurately assessing available resources ☐
Meeting deadlines ☐

Sensing whether a project or program will
     work and making appropriate recommendations ☐
Developing contingency plans in case the original
     plan doesn't work out as expected ☐
Paying attention to detail ☐

Inventing

Acting effectively on intuition ☐
Conceiving innovative methods ☐
Coming up with new ideas, new ways
     of doing things ☐
Being creative ☐

Working with figures

Numerical Skills
Solid ability with basic arithmetic ☐
Multiplying numbers in my head ☐
Numbercrunching ☐
Recognizing patterns and relationships in numbers ☐
Using graphs, tables, and charts intelligently ☐
Quickly spotting numerical errors ☐
Remembering large amounts of numerical data ☐
Analyzing statistical data ☐

Financial Skills
Understanding economic principles ☐
Raising funds ☐
Working out a budget ☐
Developing cost-cutting solutions ☐
Estimating costs ☐
Staying within budget ☐

Organizing

Organizing offices, systems, structures, layouts ☐
Setting up organizational structures
     to get things done ☐
Organizing data/information ☐
Following up on people's tasks ☐
Organizing events ☐
Making arrangements ☐
Scheduling ☐

Getting things done	Cutting through red tape	❏
	Using official channels effectively to reach goals	❏
	Keeping focused on the objective	❏
	Turning around negative situations	❏
	Effectively overseeing a highly complex situation	❏
	Handling details well without losing sight of the big picture	❏
	Processing paperwork fast	❏

COMMUNICATING

DOING: AM I GOOD AT?:

Writing	General writing ability	❏
	Writing clear, concise sentences	❏
	Grammatically correct writing	❏
	Using a wide range of vocabulary	❏
	Developing a logical, well-organized theme	❏
	Vividly describing feelings, people, senses, and things	❏
	Developing logical and persuasive points of view	❏
	Summarizing and condensing written material	❏
	Making "dry" subjects interesting	❏

The types of writing I do well:

	Informative reports	❏
	Persuasive letters	❏
	Clear memos	❏
	Well-argued policy statements	❏
	Well synthesized research reports	❏
	High quality news articles	❏
	Interesting speeches	❏
	Convincing requests for funding	❏
	Attention-getting advertising text	❏

Speaking publicly	Holding the attention of a group	❏
	Speaking clearly	❏
	Handling unexpected questions	❏
	Planning for questions that will come up	❏
	Being perceived as sincere	❏
	Making convincing arguments	❏

Presenting ideas in a logical, integrated way ☐
Poised and confident before groups ☐
Good at showmanship ☐
Responsive to audiences' moods ☐
Getting an audience involved ☐
Winning over the audience ☐

ON THE COMPUTER

DOING:	AM I GOOD AT?:	
Operating	Keying in data	☐
	Searching Internet	☐
	Handling e-mail	☐
Programming	In computer languages	☐
	Data Base Management	☐
	Statistical analysis programs	☐
	Network systems	☐
Creating	Desktop publishing documents	☐
	Powerpoint slides or datashows	☐
	Spreadsheet reports	☐
	Photofinishing and advertising	☐

It is very likely that our working list of skills left out some skills that you would like to talk about. That is only natural. Think of situations that were not covered in our list and express the skills you used in each situation you remember. Try now to think of situations which were not covered and express a skill you used in each one. A lot of such examples may come from non-job situations: volunteer work, school activities, traveling, and so on. Write down the situations and the skills you used in the following boxes.

DOING:	I WAS GOOD AT/

Grouping skills into a more meaningful portrait of yourself

Take your list of skills and group them together so they do not seem repetitive. In our long list, we have tried to be very complete. Sometimes we have given different ways of expressing what might seem to be similar skills. We did this so that you could choose whatever was closest to your own way of *seeing* your skill. Now, it is time to consolidate the skills you checked off into a *meaningful list* that helps you say something highly relevant about yourself.

For an example, below are listed some of the skills checked off by a young graduate after taking his own inventory. He wrote down:

✔ Playing as a team member

✔ Acting tactfully

✔ Being thought of as highly reliable and 'somebody you can count on'

✔ Building on others' ideas

✔ Originating ideas

✔ Seeing the value in older ways of doing things

✔ Anticipating reactions of people and sensing whether they will support a proposal

✔ Showing patience with difficult or demanding people

✔ Sensing on people's feelings, reactions, and attitudes

In reading through this list, he decided he needed to summarize it into a more general performance skill that he could easily communicate to a recruiter and offer as a benefit to the company! He looked for something that he really felt was true about himself and that he could honestly say in an interview. He summed it all up in the following way:

Growing quickly into an effective team member

This was an important discovery that could help him apply intelligently for jobs he wanted to do, and sell himself credibly! He was especially interested in applying for jobs with organizations developing their business abroad and integrating home country people and local personnel in teams that had to break into new markets and quickly ensure a viable operating unit in an untested environment. He was sure that he could work well with such teams, but didn't know exactly why. In rethinking the list of skills he had checked off, he found lots of examples from his own experience that supported this belief – as well as helping him express something *essential* about himself *succinctly*.

His next step was to build a solid case to present to a recruiter and understand the consequences of what he had found out about himself. He needed to *prove* what he said – and also understand what kinds of benefits this skill could offer!

Skill Discovery Boxes

He used a Skill Discovery Box, as shown on page 85, to: *first*, find different ways of expressing the skill; *second*, find situations in which he had already used this skill; and, *third*, imagine future situations in which he might use the skill. You can see what we wrote in the second box on page 85.

On page 86, other Skill Discovery Boxes are provided. In each box, write down the skill you believe you possess; then, write down situations where you have used this skill. Photocopy page 86, and fill in as many Skill Discovery Boxes as you need. Be very specific about the situations and just exactly what you did. This will help you prepare to write your Job Breakdowns in Chapter Four. Last, think of situations where you could use this skill to help reach results effectively. This will help you prepare an offer of services and benefits to a potential employer.

Skill Discovery Box

My skill: _____

_____

Situations where I have already used this skill	Situations in the future where I might apply this skill
_____	_____
_____	_____
_____	_____
_____	_____
_____	

This was his Skill Discovery Box

My skill: Growing quickly into an effective team member

Situations where I have already used this skill	Situations in the future where I might apply this skill
When enrolling as a member of the local Telethon Drive.	Quickly fitting in with a multinational team launching a hypermarket in Central Europe.
When successfully taking part in a business school consulting project although I had come in from another school.	Shifting from one project team to another without slowing down the new team.
Taking over for a salesman who was on summer vacation. Worked well with the other salesmen.	Taking over from an experienced team member and quickly learning his role.

Skill Discovery Box

My skill: _____

_____

Situations where I have already used this skill	Situations in the future where I might apply this skill
_____	_____
_____	_____
_____	_____
_____	_____
_____	_____

Skill Discovery Box

My skill: _____

_____

Situations where I have already used this skill	Situations in the future where I might apply this skill
_____	_____
_____	_____
_____	_____
_____	_____

How you have learned

In inventorying your personality traits and skills, you have been learning a lot about yourself. This constitutes a major step in writing your CV package, but is also preparing you to take a productive and evolutionary role in your future organization.

Learning is one of the key values in modern organizations. Old hierarchical structures are often breaking down, the speed of change is accelerating and older 'command and control' organizations are becoming 'learning organizations'. It is said that, in the future, people will not have 'jobs' but rather 'work'; they should not think of themselves as fitting into a specialized career, but constantly participating in the creation of value within structures in a constant state of flux. 'Life-long learning' will become the rule.

> We pay great attention to what applicants have done before. We believe that we can determine how successful people will be based on what they have done in the past. It is not so much a question of having succeeded, but rather of having learned. We feel 'learners' and 'adapters' will be with us in 20 or more years, therefore 'what' they have achieved is certainly important, but, above all, 'how' they have achieved it.
> **Valerie Robert, Procter & Gamble**

This is already occurring as the information technology revolution facilitates the disintegration of old structures and favors the forming, un-forming, and reforming of project teams. No wonder that all recruiters stress the need for people who can learn and learn and learn! You must be ready to show your awareness of having learned in the past. You must also be aware of *how* you learned. This is important in order to communicate your capability of learning in the future.

Understanding your own learning process

In this Chapter so far, you have been reliving situations so that you could *see* your skills. This has helped you a great deal in your ability to *voice* what you do well. On the other hand, on the job, in the situations you have inventoried, your learning process was probably closer to the acquisition of reflexes, ways of acting, a kind of 'dexterity in doing'; this is typically what we call 'being experienced'.

Yet, doing is not sufficient to produce benefits; benefits are results! Understanding what you have learned has a great deal to do with the results you reached, the outcomes you produced.

In the following pages, we are going to explore some key concepts in management-like problems, outcomes and accomplishments – to help you make an offer of benefits to an organization that you can back up!

What you have done

For recruiters there is a strong link between what you have done and what you can do. Using skills should lead to results. As said before, all companies hire problem-solvers, and the clearest results are the solutions to problems. What kinds of problems have you solved?

Showing that your skills produce results

Re-read your past and think about what experiences you felt should go on your CV. Why should they go there? Do they demonstrate the skills you have inventoried? How do you show these skills in a CV? The answer is quite simple: by showing problems you have solved using those skills, by showing accomplishments achieved with those skills.

Although the answer is simple, writing in a way which clearly conveys the challenges you overcame, so that the employer can see your skills, is not necessarily so simple!

Understanding the concepts of problems and accomplishments[6]

Problems

Managers say they spend about 70% of their time solving problems. Yet, many also say that the most difficult thing is to recognize what the problem is. They know they have a problem, but they don't know what it is![7] Much of the confusion comes from using the word too

---

6 See Interview with Valerie Robert, *Procter and Gamble*, Chapter 4, page 112.

loosely in everyday speech. We say "I have a problem with a customer," "there's a problem of communication," or "the problem is to find out..." These abuses of language may be fine in relaxed conversation but are no help at all in solving the problem. In management, there is a very useful definition of a problem that helps us avoid the kind of confusion that comes from careless use of the word: "a problem is a discrepancy between an existing and a desired [situation]".[8] In other words, "what I want to be happening is not". Another good definition along the same lines is: "a problem is a blocked managerial objective".

All of these definitions suggest one powerful logic: we have to know what the "desired state of affairs" is, i.e., the "objective". What was the organization trying to accomplish that you were helping with? This will be taken up in detail in Chapter Four when you are writing your Work Experience section or dealing with your accomplishments and achievements. For the time being, remember that when you want to talk about a problem you solved, you must be able to communicate the objective of the organization.

A fishbone chart is often a good thinking device for reviewing problems you have dealt with in the past. It allows you to start with the problems – such as poor output, insufficient sales, late deliveries – and trace them directly back to their causes. Were the causes manpower, machines, methods or materials? Analyzing your experiences using this approach will help you make palpable the actions you were taking in dealing with the problems you solved. That, in turn, will allow you to write dense, clear sentences showing the causes you were acting on, and, thus, the skills you were using.

---

7 See the *One Minute Manager*, Kenneth Blanchard.
  Also available in French: *Le Manager minute*, Éditions d'Organisation, 1987.
8 *Management, Robbins*, Stephen and Coulter, Mary, Sixth Edition, Prentice Hall, 1999, p.151.

The Fishbone Chart

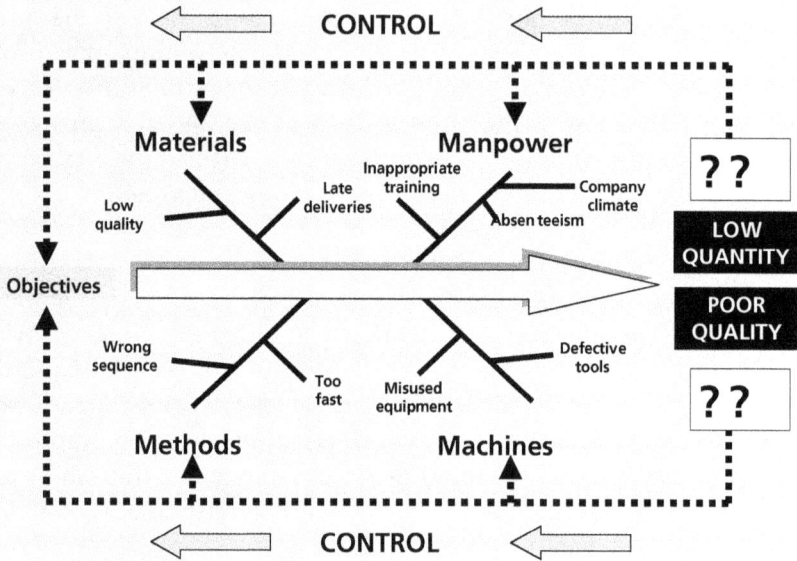

CONTROL

Materials

Manpower

Low quality

Late deliveries

Inappropriate training

Company climate

Absenteeism

Objectives

? ?

LOW QUANTITY

POOR QUALITY

Wrong sequence

Too fast

Misused equipment

Defective tools

? ?

Methods

Machines

CONTROL

Source: unknown

Accomplishments

Whether you call them results, outcomes, accomplishments, or achievements, they are all something you did personally that improved a situation or made a contribution that you should be proud of. We say 'should', because you may be modest, or not have thought about being proud of them yet, at least to the point of mentioning them in a CV. Like skills, accomplishments come from on-the-job activities, outside activities, hobbies and school. Accomplishments come from outcomes you generated when you overcame a problem, possibly in response to a goal you set for yourself. Company application forms or recruiters in interviews will often ask you to talk about challenges you have set for yourself and what the outcomes were. This is another inventory you should draw up: a list of accomplishments you are proud of. This is an inventory closely linked with the personality traits and skills inventories you have already made.

To give you an idea of what accomplishments look like, we are providing a small sampling of real accomplishments our graduates have put on their CVs over the years. Many of these are 'off-the-job' achievements. What links all these accomplishments is the simple sense of pride of having made a serious contribution to something.

- Bilingual medical interpreter at a two-day conference on the installation of a new research scanner at the district hospital
- Carried out start-to-finish market research for variety of companies through our student-run Marketing Service
- Designed a promotion leaflet, contacted professional magazines and planned an advertising campaign
- Designed the layout for and word-processed a student-published guide of the region
- Founded a student investment club at my school
- Raised sufficient funding to finance a short subject film festival
- Oversaw the organization of a series of conferences given by local business leaders at my university
- Set up 3 local branches of the national Hunger Project in our region for collecting and distributing free take-away meals to needy people

Remember your accomplishments can come from anywhere, working alone or with others. You should imagine for a moment that you are sitting through an interview with a recruiter who asks you to remember some of your major accomplishments. Use the following preparation sheet to help you get ready to explain what you did for each accomplishment.

YOUR ACCOMPLISHMENT

1. What was the challenge or the problem to overcome?

2. What exactly did you do that you are proud of?

3. What skills did you use?

4. What benefits were produced?

LINK THE JOB, THE COMPANY AND YOURSELF

Now your inventory should be complete. With your major personality traits described, your skills pinned down and a list of accomplishments you would be glad to talk to someone about, you are ready to start thinking about how you are going to write your CV. You may have many skills and many accomplishments, but, like a good salesman who has listened carefully to his customer's problems and needs, you are not necessarily going to put everything about yourself on the table. You are going to have to choose from what you have done, and can do, with what needs to be done! The employer wants to get a succinct 'picture' of the benefits you can offer *him*, not an endless list of skills and accomplishments. He wants you to be able to organize this portrait of yourself so that he can understand it. He wants you to know both yourself and his organization – and make the match yourself.[9]

The first part of the 'picture' which makes the match for him is the CV itself, which acts as a *pre-interview*! In the CV you are going to describe what you have already done and accomplished, thus showing your skills. But to do it well, you should understand the different kind of interview techniques that are used by recruiters to put together what they feel is an accurate portrait of the applicant. In our opinion, the only approach to interviewing that can be carried over to CV-writing is behavioral interviewing and open-ended questions. But to understand why, let's review the different techniques.

---

9 See Interview with Philippe Gracia, *Auchan Hypermarkets*, Chapter 4, page 110.

```
        ┌──────────────┐
        │     THE      │
        │   PORTRAIT   │
        │      OF      │
        │   YOURSELF   │
        └──────────────┘

┌──────────────┐        ↑        ┌──────────────┐
│     THE      │        │        │     THE      │
│  NATURE OF   │   ◄────┼────►   │   COMPANY:   │
│   THE JOB    │        │        │  BUSINESS &  │
└──────────────┘                 │   CULTURE    │
                                 └──────────────┘
```

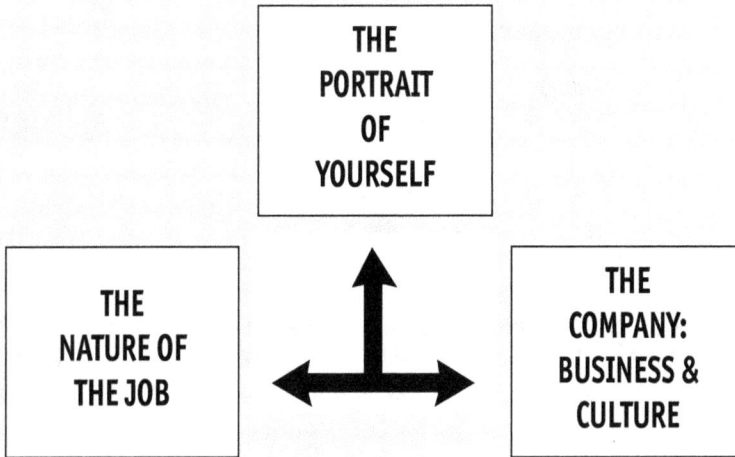

INTERVIEW #4:
KNOW YOURSELF
AND THE COMPANY

Interview with Laurent Yvon, Vice President Human Resources Europe, Hilti Corporation, Liechtenstein.

▶ **Could you give us an overview of Hilti's recruiting process?**

We use a variety of avenues to pull in young talent. We have developed a partnership with the CEMS (Community of European Management Schools), an organization grouping 16 European Management schools, all delivering the same standard education. This guarantees us applicants with a solid educational background in marketing, management, organizing, planning, etc. We also count on our own subsidiaries to shortlist a number of applicants each year, coming from different schools (universities, business and technical schools).

After this pre-selection process – done in all cases in English – applicants are then invited to attend a two-day seminar with Hilti managers at what we call our 'incubators', or assessment centers, where we probe the 'soft' competencies that really make the difference between our candidates. The CV is important at the initial step but takes its full value when the candidates selected from the seminars move on to the next stage.

▶ What are Hilti's key recruitment criteria?

As I have described above, applicants have all been pre-selected by their education; they all have the same basic know-how, the 'hard' skills. We are particularly interested in several other factors:

- The 'soft' competencies I have mentioned: We call them *Master Competencies*. To name a few: *Accurate understanding of people*: this is essential for persons who will work their whole life long with customers and subordinates. *Self confidence:* we want people who are confident in a variety of situations, who know how not to be 'shaky.' *Pride and pro-active behavior:* people who take pride in what they do, who care, and who seek out and solve problems before they occur. We also know that **communication** is a key factor in the lives of our future employees, and we seek to determine if they have this 'soft' skill.

- The cultural 'fit': Our motto might be: "forget the job, get a career". We recruit for the long-term. Our corporate culture is very strong; people have to feel they share our values. At the same time, we consciously aim for a certain diversity, we do not want *clones*.

- Languages: Our young talents are all trilingual. International mobility is a necessity for us. We are growing fast, establishing ourselves all over the world, and due to our values and the complexity of our business, we need to develop our managers from within. So our people will need to speak several languages well. Before becoming a sales manager in Germany, you might typically be a salesman in France. We check applicants' language ability carefully.

- International exposure: We want our young applicants to have already made the first steps to internationalize themselves, with a traineeship period or some education abroad. We believe the schools have all provided the same education, so the difference is often made by this international exposure.

- Self-awareness: This is absolutely the key factor. It is very difficult to over-emphasize it. Candidates need to know their own skills, know who they are and what they like. They need to couple that with knowledge about us, to know if they would be happy working with us. Both Hilti and the new recruit are going to make a serious investment. A mistake can have very serious consequences for them both.

▶ What role does the applicant's CV play in your recruiting process?

Both the letter and CV are important at different stages of the selection process. In the CV, we look for much more than an established model; we want the CV and letter to be clear, precise and honest! CVs that go on and on, that are too long, are unbearable. We don't have the time and long CVs are not appealing. We are going to spend one minute on the CV and when it is too long, you start to ask yourself: "What does he want, I don't understand, I don't see what he has achieved. What is he or she aiming for?" Then we can conclude the applicant is not interesting for us, he doesn't know what he wants to do, and, in any case, does not know how to express himself clearly. Once again what counts is self awareness, knowing what and who one is. You can't please everybody, so be yourself! Different people may have lived through similar experiences, but some may have seen a challenge in a situation and sought to overcome it. This is the person we want! Not all of these experiences should be looked for in professional life; very often young people find out what they are through extra-curricular experiences. Originality at any cost is really not important in a CV. You don't know who's going to read it anyway.

▶ What about the letter?

I find that the letter, particularly a hand-written one, is a very cultural phenomenon. In France, and perhaps England, it remains very important. It many countries it doesn't exist in its hand-written form. Yet, it is true that it is an important communication too that too many do without. It provides a 'magnifying glass' through which we can see what the applicant wants to do, what he or she is looking for, his or her career plan! Above all, it should be sincere!

Many of our applicants now send Internet CVs and add 10 to 15 lines of introduction where they explain why they are coming to us. This is good, because they tell us what they are aiming at.

▶ What do you look for in the interview?

At the interview, self-awareness and knowledge of the company become crucial. We check for the 'fit'. Too often we find out the applicants don't know themselves and haven't taken the time to understand who we are. If you apply in a 'process-oriented' company, as an applicant you have to ask yourself: "Would I be happy in a process-based company?" We are in a company where we live change as an opportunity to grow and develop individuals. As a candidate, you have to ask yourself if you are able to live change. You have to be prepared to face new challenges, to take risks and to benefit from new experiences and new opportunities. That's an aspect I probe for seriously during the interview. I ask them, "Can you imagine us working together?" Sometimes, we meet applicants that have never checked our Internet sites to better understand what we produce and market; it's a surprise for us. On the other hand, we meet people who have done their "homework" before the interview – visiting one of our stores for example. These applicants are giving themselves a greater chance to be successful.

GET READY FOR THE INTERVIEW

If the CV is a pre-interview, you should write yours in a way to answer the questions that will be asked.

Hypothetical questions

Hypothetical questions are often used by interviewers. These kinds of questions ask what you would do in certain situations. These may be situations you have never faced before. Often such questions only measure the applicant's cleverness and encourage him to 'psyche out' the interviewer, to guess what he wants to hear. Typically applicants try to give the answer they feel the company wants. Questions might range from:

> *"What would you do if you caught someone stealing from the company and you knew that he had financial problems?"*
> to
> *"How would you go about trying to change a policy that your boss supported but that you felt was detrimental to the department's operations?"*

We feel hypothetical questions are often over-used by poor interviewers. Such questions may be asked to check a candidate's resourcefulness or creativity under pressure; they may even be good at assessing managerial scope, but they are poor at verifying real performance skills. They do not seek evidence that the applicant has had actual experience with such matters. If they are followed up by behavioral interviewing, however, they may be very powerful. One way or the other, they are difficult to *pre-answer* in a CV, since a CV deals with "what I have already done, or am doing".

Closed-ended or 'Yes or no' questions

Questions requiring yes or no answers are often sprinkled throughout an interview, to check factual information, to compare your profile with the job description or to refocus the interview on the concrete if it has been drifting off course through light conversation, joking or exchange of opinion. The best way to prepare for such questions is to have a mastery of your own background. You should have already acquired a certain mastery of that background in your preparation in this chapter, a mastery you will strengthen in chapter Four.

Behavioral interviewing and open-ended questions

Importance of the past to predict the future

Many modern behavioral interviewing techniques are based on using past behavior as indicators of how a person will perform in the future. Although interviewers are aware that such techniques are far from foolproof, they feel that probing the interviewee for examples of specific behavior will provide information that will allow them to accurately assess the person's skills for specific situations he or she is likely to encounter in the new job. This technique avoids 'what if' questions, unless they are related to a specific example of behavior in the applicant's past. The interviewer is essentially building a 'case' that proves that the applicant is what he or she claims to be. The past events that are scrutinized in such interviewing become 'evidence', positive or negative, of the skills the applicant is offering.

Open-ended questions

Open-ended questions are the most commonly used questions in behavioral interviewing techniques and are often launched by a closed-ended question. Typical examples are:

"Did you enjoy your last job?"

This is typically followed by "Why?" The information given in the "Why" part of the answer provides the richest information to the interviewer.

Almost all open-ended questions aim at gathering information on the past behavior of the applicant, his or her performance and attitudes. Such questions go far beneath the surface and invite applicants to develop full portraits of themselves. The way a person has dealt with instructions, responsibilities, information and people in specific situations provides great insight into what might be expected in the future from the same person. When confronted with highly targeted questioning about past experience, the thoughtful applicant will rarely fall silent (except to think) and will always have an eventual reaction to the interviewer's questions, because he will have thought about the purposefulness of what he or she had done and will have developed a certain perspective. The unthoughtful applicant will be caught unaware and will stop dead in the interview, suddenly finding himself at a loss. To the interviewer, this will simply indicate a lack of analysis and commitment to the job.

Penetration technique

The penetration technique is merely a variation on behaviorial interviewing, used for probing a given area in greater depth. It uses *layers* of open-ended questions pushing the interviewee into more and more detail, allowing the interviewer to zoom in on the skills and personality traits he wants to discover. It typically might run like this:

> *"What do you feel was your best contribution to the department in which you last worked?"*
>
> *"Why was it better than other things you did?"*
>
> *"Did you have any difficulty getting it accepted?"*
>
> *"Why did you?"*
>
> *"How did you overcome those difficulties?"*
>
> *"What did you learn from the experience that might help you if you join our company?"*

A Special Interview: the Case Interview

The Case Interview is often used by consulting firms. The interviewee is given a business case, possibly a strategy case like those used in business schools and MBA programs. The case in not very long and the interviewee will be asked to react quickly orally to the questions of the interviewer. Often the candidate will be asked to summarize the problems of the company in question, give an analysis and suggest solutions. He or she will be expected to defend the logic of the solutions proposed.

Now that we have reviewed the different interview techniques, you are ready to write your CV as an interview you can control – with Chapter Four!

© Éditions d'Organisation

Key points in chapter three

- You need to find out everything you can about the job you are applying for.

- You need to find out everything about the company you are applying to.

- You have to find out everything you can about **yourself**.

- Think like a salesman.

- What is it that the company wants done that you can do?

- Understand what skills are.

- Make a complete list of your skills.

- Group your skills into a portrait of what kind of person you are to work with.

- Faites des recherches très complètes sur le poste que vous souhaitez occuper avant de postuler.

- Vous devez tout savoir sur l'entreprise où vous postulez.

- Apprenez à bien **vous** connaître.

- Pensez en vendeur.

- Cherchez à identifier ce dont l'entreprise a besoin et ce que vous pouvez faire pour elle.

- Comprenez bien ce que "compétence" signifie.

- Faites une liste exhaustive de vos compétences.

- Regroupez vos compétences de sorte à montrer le type de personne que vous êtes au travail.

- Understand the concept of results and accomplishments.

- Make a clear link between the company, the job and yourself.

- Prepare for the different kinds of interview questions before you write your CV.

- Comprenez bien ce que résultats et accomplissements signifient pour l'entreprise où vous postulez.

- Etablissez un lien très clair entre vous-même, l'entreprise et l'emploi auquel vous postulez

- Avant de rédiger votre CV préparez-vous aux différents type de questions posées en entretien.

What to show in a CV

Above all, you must remember that the CV acts as a kind of interview. Until the hirer meets you in person, it is the only chance that he or she has to get to know you. What makes hiring people so difficult is that we have seldom worked along beside them, seen them perform, or solved problems with them. Despite the most sophisticated testing and cross-interviewing techniques, almost any interviewer would like to be able to become invisible for a day in order to observe you on the job. In your CV, you should make every effort to help the interviewer to get a good idea of how you perform! To do this, you should remember the kinds of interviews we have described in Chapter Three and *pre-answer* some of the questions the interviewer would like to ask you.

Pretend you are sitting in front of the interviewer. Live through the questioning by thinking like a manager and understanding what managers look for. As you actually sit for more and more interviews you will, of course, become much better at writing your CV as a first interview because you will grasp their way of looking *into* the world in which you were operating. Learning to open the door to that world and providing the CV-reader with clear insight into your skills and performance as though you were talking to him face-to-face can tip the balance in your favor and ensure you an actual interview. On the other hand, applicants who write CVs that are vague, full of generalities, and unfocused are keeping the door to their experience closed. This only irritates the employer who is looking for a "fleshed-out", three-dimensional portrait of the job-seeker. Recruiters will toss such 'flat' pictures into the trash and choose those CVs that make them feel like wanting to know the writer better.

WRITE YOUR CV AS AN INTERVIEW

All interviewing techniques aim to determine how an applicant will perform in certain circumstances. We have discussed these techniques in Chapter Three. We will base our writing on behavioral interviewing, which probes the applicant's past behavior to determine how he or she will perform in the future. This is logical, since applicants cannot answer hypothetical questions or 'yes or no' questions on a CV. However, you need to understand what recruiters are really trying to find out in probing your past actions and outcomes. You will understand management and communication better! Above all, you will understand better the links between *what you have done and what you can do*!

| What you have done | ⟹ | What you can do! |

Recognizing the links between what you did and your skills, the contexts in which you used them, your personal job preferences and your future aspirations will allow you to fit everything together into a well thought-out CV package that ties in with a career plan you can manage.

Write your own 'open-ended questions'

As we can see, open-ended questions aim at having you clearly describe a situation in which you have made a contribution. This is essential! Greater information about the context in which you acted helps communicate a great deal about the skills you used, as well as about your personal qualities. Let the employer get a good look at *your understanding* of what was at stake.

Remember the definition of management as "getting things done through other people". Most often than not, as a trainee, intern or assistant, you were one of the 'people' who things were getting '*done through*'. Showing awareness of how your actions fit into 'the big picture' of the organization's functioning and goals goes a long way towards communicating your potential for growth and future management responsibility. If you have been in a position where you were assigning, delegating, supervising or informing others, then, in a pure sense, you were acting as a manager. If that is true, much of your own contribution will come from how well you explained 'the big picture' to others!

In any case, whether on the receiving or the giving side of instructions, you will be expected to be able to explain the importance of what was happening and your role in it. Learn to write your own open-ended questions about your different accomplishments so that you can answer them yourself and gain complete knowledge of yourself and what you have done. Often interviewers will ask you to relive a situation thoroughly. '*Play a little movie in your mind*', they will say, to force you to retrace your steps. If you understand management and business well enough, you will be able to deduce the kinds of information they need to assess a potential coworker. Then you will be able to draw up a performance assessment on yourself as if you were your own boss.

In the list below, look at the examples of questions that any interviewer might ask to get a clearer understanding of your skills.

Play a little movie in your mind

Typical open-ended questions might run like this.

- Tell me about a time when you had to deal with a difficult customer who was upset. How did you deal with it exactly?

- Describe a situation where you had to build on a pre-existing filing system that was functioning poorly, without sacrificing its qualities.

- Tell me about a situation where you made a major contribution to the running of a department or a student association. How did you do this?

- Describe a time when you were given a free hand to revamp something. How did you deal with it?

- Tell me about a co-worker or fellow student with whom you were having considerable difficulty getting the job done. What were the causes and how did you handle it?

- Describe a time when you had to report on major business developments in your industry to aid in decision-making. How did you go about it? What kind of information did you gather? How did you write and present the report? What were its weaknesses?

Questions like those above are aimed at forcing the applicant to 'relive' an experience in great enough detail for the interviewer to be able to understand exactly what skills the person used in the situation. To get a clearer idea of what he might find out from the applicant, look below to see what might constitute typical answers to those sample questions:

Typical answers might run like this.

- Tell me about a time when you had to deal with a difficult customer who was upset. How did you deal with it exactly?

A major customer threatened to withdraw his business over delivery delays of a batch of parts crucial to his scheduled production. I followed the matter up and found that our own suppliers were late in delivery.
I contacted an Internet part services supplier and organized an emergency delivery for the customer.

- Describe a situation where you had to build on a pre-existing filing system that was functioning poorly, without sacrificing its qualities.

Assigned to updating a prospect list for a real estate developer, I found that the base failed to include income levels and commuting distances to work.
I managed to integrate these criteria, without a time-consuming rebuilding of the base. Then I telephoned many of the prospects and updated their files. This also helped increase visits to our model homes.

- Tell me about a situation where you made a major contribution to the running of a department or student association. How did you do this?

In our school art and document reproduction service, I initiated a new scheduling policy which doubled the number of hours the service was available for students.

- Describe a time when you were given a free hand to revamp something. How did you deal with it?

Hired as a new clerk in a wines and spirits store, I asked the owner if I could make some suggestions on window display and store layout to set off products better. After two weeks, the customers complimented the new organization, and our sales of better vintage wines and fine liqueurs increased by 30%.

- Tell me about a co-worker or fellow student with whom you were having considerable difficulty getting the job done. What were the causes and how did you handle it?

As a young assistant, I perceived that an experienced, up-from-the-ranks employee was resisting some of my suggestions. Feeling that my university education was irritating to her, I began to ask her opinion on much of what I was doing. This later led to her welcoming many of my ideas and helped me succeed in my job in the department.

- Describe a time when you had to report on major business developments in your industry to aid in decision-making. How did you go about it? What kind of information did you gather? How did you write and present the report? What were its weaknesses?

Left very much on my own, I searched on Internet and found many sources. Yet I lacked a clear idea of how to prepare such a report. I questioned several of my older colleagues, found additional sources in local library press reviews and worked out a good structure for making the report clear. I also read articles to help me prepare an oral presentation. Although my report was succinct, it was said that it was too long and the conclusions were not 'upfront'. I was congratulated on the quality of my presentation.

Good answers suggest skills

All of these answers have one thing in common: they give the interviewer insight into the applicants' skills. The interviewees have been thoughtful enough, gone into enough detail, and possess enough self-knowledge to allow the interviewer to see their skills and character traits. The above answers have already been transformed somewhat from spoken style to written style, although they still need reorganization to constitute good 'entries' on a CV. *Above all, they provide information about specific actions taken in concrete contexts.* This information might never have been provided by an applicant if the questions had not been asked. Our responsibility in writing is to interview ourselves, and for that we have to understand what recruiters want from people, and we have to have a clear awareness – well-documented – of our own worth!

Let's re-read the answers and make a list of the skills and personality traits that come across through the above answers:

	Skills communicated	**Character traits**
Question One	Responsibility-taking, follow-through	Initiative, thoroughness
Question Two	Analysis, contact	Planning, independence
Question Three	Inventiveness, needs analysis	Far-sightedness, involvement
Question Four	Inventiveness, analysis	Assertiveness, tact
Question Five	Rapport-building, learning	Sensitivity, tact
Question Six	Researching, writing, learning, follow-through, self-criticism, initiative	Independence, humility, ambition

As we said in Chapter Three, it is sometimes difficult to separate skills from character traits. It is not really necessary to do so; it might turn out to be a sterile exercise for our purposes, which are to paint a portrait of ourselves as a kind of person to work with and work alongside. 'Playing the little *movie'* will go a long way to helping us do just that!

Put a 'movie' on paper

How do we go about *filming* situations like those described above to create the pre-interview that is rich in information about ourselves? The secret is a series of steps that have a lot to do with understanding management. Through these steps we can

> We feel a mature and intelligent applicant should be able to play a clearly reasoned 'movie' to us that sets out his development and the contributions he can make in about 10 minutes without breaking the story line.
> **Philippe Gracia, Auchan**

learn to break down our various experiences into essential components that, when brought together in a dense but complete description, communicate a maximum amount in information about our essential nature.

Everyone points out the need to be 'brief'. We often forget the other half, which is to be 'clear and to the point.' Virtual reality can only be created through detail. Saying the essential is different from brevity in itself. Short is not the same as interesting. Obviously we are not trying to make a full-length feature, but we are trying to get across something 'telling' about certain of our experiences. Let's work through a management analysis process to help us focus on what is *telling* for professional business people.

INTERVIEW #5 :
PLAY A 'MOVIE' TO THE RECRUITER

Interview with Philippe Gracia, Human Resource Manager, Auchan Hypermarkets, Poland

▶ **How should candidates approach the application process?**

First of all, whether they are students seeking an internship or graduates applying for a full-time job, they should *not* approach it like college kids preparing for exams. They are not writing or talking to us to take a test! Young people applying for a job with us should keep in mind that the company is recruiting because it has plans for development. They should ask to play a part in that development, to satisfy the company's needs, and not to fulfill their own expectations. Our role will be to help these young people grow in the right direction so as to be a productive member of the firm, develop on the job and acquire the qualities that will allow them to have rewarding careers with us.

▶ **What qualities do you look for in an applicant?**

One of the most important aspects is self-knowledge. Successful applicants must know themselves thoroughly. They will have to recruit themselves first. They will have performed a full and sincere self-assessment, know what interests them, just how it interests them and why! They should be able to make an offer of services, to tell us exactly what they can contribute to, how they can do that and prove they can do it because of what they have learned. It is up to the applicants themselves to tell us what their qualities are and why they want a certain job. Above all, candidates must be able to provide us with insight into their personalities through the things that interest them. All of this should be communicated in a well-structured and concise approach.

Knowing how to focus on the essential is a quality we feel is very important. When we recruit graduates from top business schools, we are sure that they have developed their analytical and thinking skills and fine-tuned their ability to get to the heart of the matter. On the other hand, too few applicants have really taken the responsibility for their own recruitment, because they have not thought it through. We feel a mature and intelligent applicant should be able to play a clearly reasoned 'movie' to us that sets out his development and the contributions he can make in about 10 minutes without breaking the story line.

A company recruiter is an extension of the company rather than an independent agent; he breathes the very culture of his firm into the recruitment process. Applicants must correspond to that culture. At Auchan, we want young people who are dynamic, outward-going and committed to the general good. They should know that their involvement in the firm's life will be rewarded by an integration in a real community of interests: our firm wants its employees to like their jobs. The successful candidate at Auchan must be a salesman, must like to buy and sell – because we are in sales. He or she should be someone who understands and tackles operational problems but also able to dream about the future of the company –"with his feet in the mud and his head in the stars."

▶ **What other advice do you have to give to applicants?**

First, never lie! Don't try to be too original either; too much originality can 'kill' a CV, unless you are sure about the recruiter's sense of humor. Develop your internships and summer jobs that have a relationship with the business of the company. There should be a logic to a CV, where everything has some link to the job being sought.

WRITING A CV IS UNDERSTANDING MANAGEMENT

Whether or not you have studied strategic analysis, management problem-solving and MBO[1] techniques, the following paragraphs will talk about these management tools and link them specifically with ways you can use to enhance your communication about your own problem-solving background and capabilities.

Showing your understanding of the part you played in the organization

As pointed out in Chapter Two, people don't really hire *people*, they hire *problem-solvers*. Although they might select you partly on the basis of a 'likable' personality, this is so they can work with you better, and

---

1 *Management by Objectives.* A technique invented by Peter Drucker in his 1954 book the *Practice of Management.* MBO refers to a set of procedures that runs from goal setting through performance review. Central to the method is the working out of clear objectives through negotiation between managers and subordinates. Drucker suggested that managers at every level help set the objectives for levels higher than their own. This was to give them a better understanding of the broader strategy of the company and how their own specific objectives related to the overall picture.

so get the problems solved more easily. Defining people and 'likability' is outside the scope of this book. However, understanding problems and methods of solving them is decidedly within its scope. If you have experience to communicate, it is certainly in the field of problem-solving.

Good problem-solvers are inevitably 'involved' people; they tend to get profoundly interested in the problem they are working on, curious about everything pertaining to it, hungry for information and detail that will help them wrap it up. Modern organizations spend a great deal of time and money trying to gain 'commitment' from their personnel, commitment to the organization's objectives. Involvement and commitment are very close to each other. If they can measure your ability to get involved, they are that much closer to finding the person they want to solve their problems. Showing involvement has a lot to do with detailed information and your *understanding* of the organization's goals.

INTERVIEW #6 :
THE IMPORTANCE OF PAST ACTION

Interview with Valerie Robert, Human Resource Manager, Procter & Gamble, London

▶ **What key aspects of an applicant do you hope to discover in a CV?**

At Procter, the selection process is crucial because we promote internally. If we make a mistake in recruitment, we have lost a sizeable investment and, as well, locked out a valuable candidate. We pay great attention to what applicants have done before. We believe that we can determine how successful people will be based on what they have done in the past. It is not so much a question of having succeeded, but rather of having learned. We feel 'learners' and 'adapters' will be with us in 20 or more years, therefore 'what' they have achieved is certainly important, but, above all, 'how' they have achieved it. We look for what we call '*what counts*' factors, among which are problem-solving, ability to communicate, working with others, initiative and follow-through.

▶ **In your opinion, what are the major difficulties applicants experience in writing a CV and Letter?**

Above all, being specific! Applicants talk about *activities*, but what we want to see is *actions* they have taken to reach *outcomes*. The CV should be action-oriented. Specificity is all the more important as each P&G department hires for itself. Although the Human Resource Department provides training in recruitment to other departments, it does not hire for those departments. This means the CV should show something real about the accomplishments of the person. As a first step in the recruiting process, the CV provides the only way we have to catch a glimpse of the skills of the person writing. We see these skills through the *actions* they have taken. Too often, candidates will say things like "I work well with others", but they provide no proof, no examples of specific situations.

▶ **What are some of the most important traits you look for?**

Applicants should know themselves and where they want to go. Self-knowledge is absolutely the key! Without this, they cannot measure the 'fit' between themselves and the company. This means they also need to know the company well, to have done their research and to have thought through whether they belong with us. For example, trust and integrity are key values at P&G. That is another reason we want detailed information and specifics. Applicants should also think about what they want to be *doing* in the future – not something like "I like travelling and people." They should think in terms of 'deliverables'– what they can produce. In short, they should have done their homework about themselves and the company.

▶ **How long do you think a CV should be?**

One page, no more. We feel that an applicant should have thought enough about what he has done to be able to communicate the essential on one page. Otherwise, we don't feel the learning has taken place.

Showing involvement through an understanding of the organization's goals

Understanding an organization's goals is not abstract; it is closely related to our understanding of why we are doing what we are doing. It makes the difference between someone working like an automaton and a creator. Yet, you may be a creator and communicate like an automaton! Let's look at some examples of that. Below we have two versions of a fictional conversation between husband and wife that takes place when the wife, who works at City Hall, steps in the door after work:

Version 1 ➤ **COMPARE WITH** ➤ **Version 2**

"How was your day, Honey?"	"How was your day, Honey?"
"All right"	"All right"
"What did you do?"	"What did you do?"
"Oh, I answered the phone, wrote a couple of reports and met with the mayor for an hour."	"Well, I helped some new-comers to the district enroll their children in the local school, drafted one report on the need for new census takers and another on the frequent complaints about our slow building permit process. Then I briefed the mayor on the backlogs of work piling up, that our staff was not managing to process."

Of course, this is caricatural, but it does demonstrate how information communicates involvement. The first conversation suggests boredom, routine – an automaton executing tasks. The second shows someone who knows, cares, is interested. The first also suggests the person doesn't like his job. The second suggests someone committed, who understands what the City Hall is trying to get done, who is definitely a problem-solver. Same person, same job – different communication!

Fans of brevity will be afraid that the second version is too long for a CV and certainly not dense enough in information content. It might be pointed out that, although not written in scannable style, the second version takes very little room. If we try to fit it into a well-structured Chronological CV, for example,

It takes this much room!

Over the years, we have asked participants in our CV-writing seminars to come back after the first session with 'job breakdowns' of every job they have ever had. As a starting point, they are supposed to break the jobs down into at least four different tasks and use an appropriate action verb for each. Often their first version completely lacks life because it is poor in information. Although the purpose of asking them to do this is to find out something about their past that makes them interesting, the effect is often the opposite. A typical case we often refer to was of a very gifted trainee from a business school who nevertheless brought back the following poor job breakdown:

Very little information!

- Wrote letters
- Answered phone
- Tested software
- Dealt with suppliers

This provided much too little information to a recruiter trying to make a choice of whether to interview this person for a job or not. Using her case as an example in the seminar, we probed for more information about each of the four entries she had written. We suspected from the beginning that the last two – "tested software" and "dealt with suppliers" – probably had the richest problem-solving content, but we were not sure. With the help of the other participants, we were able to bring out what was really important in her work experience and write a job breakdown that demonstrated her project management skills.

This was her rewritten version

Trial-tested custom-designed accounting software package for suitability and reported deficiencies to developer for improvement. System now in use and operating efficiently.

The new version provided a clear picture of what was really her greatest responsibility during this summer job. The employer learns that she was entrusted with important decisions for the company and that she handled relations with the supplier company. The seminar participants were able to get the information they wanted through a series of questions. The process of questioning went much like this:

Our questions	Her answers	What we learnt
• What was the most interesting part of your job?	Oh, testing the software- by far!	We had thought it might be dealing with suppliers.
• Why was it?	Because I was given full responsibility for the assignment.	We realized she was given latitude to handle it.
• What kind of software was it?	Software to handle all the company's accounting.	It could have been for word-processing and given another conception of her skills.

Our questions	Her answers	What we learnt
• Was it a retail, ready-made software program?	Oh, no. It had been designed for the company over a period of six months. It was very expensive.	We thought it was standard. This increased our understanding of the importance of her work.
• Why did he ask you to test it?	I knew accounting and software pretty well and the company manager told me to take care of it.	We get a better picture of a double competence.
• What do you mean by test?	He wanted me to run it through all the operations we usually performed and see if it met our needs.	Furnished an even better idea of her skills.
• What did you learn about the software?	In many ways, it did not do the things we wanted it to do, particularly in cross-referencing.	Gave us a look at her capability and judgment
• Did you report all this to your boss, orally or in writing?	Neither. He told me to make the decisions and deal directly with the developer to make sure the changes were made.	We didn't expect this. It showed her level of empowerment.
• Were the changes made and did it work?	I don't know. I finished my traineeship and went back to school.	This meant she didn't know the outcome of her work. It was essential for her to find out. We all suggested she call the company and ask if the system was working well after her management of the project. She did.
• After calling the company to follow up on the trial-testing, she was able to report:	They said I had done a good job and the system was working well.	We now know her performance was good.

If we look at her final job breakdown, we find that she has carefully selected a series of adjectives, more carefully chosen her verbs and tried to "put us into the picture." She has also thought in management terms, by building in information about the objectives of the company and the outcomes of her work.

Company objectives   **Company objectives**

Trial-tested custom-designed accounting software package for suitability and reported deficiencies to developer for improvement. System now in use and operating efficiently.

Outcome

In thinking in terms of objectives and outcomes, she has perceived of herself as an actor in a process. She is taking a management perspective and using her conceptual skills to see the 'bigger picture' or the overview of an organizational process and her role in it. By doing this, she is thinking more like a manager than like just 'a cog in a machine'.

Understanding yourself as an actor in a process

Process thinking and systems logic are basic to management. Businesses have been going through a re-engineering of their value chains and processes to streamline relationships between the different parts of their organization and produce greater efficiency. The rise of lateral teams, systems integration and network structures requires employees that understand how all parts fit together in a smoothly functioning 'whole'. For this, conceptual skills and the ability to constantly change have become the 'core competencies' expected of managers and workers alike.

In writing your CV, you should rethink your past experience as though you were managing a process. Imagine yourself as part of a flowchart in Operations Management. You are the processor through which inputs are turned into outputs. At a glance, the recruiter should be able to see an active, corporate, performance-oriented individual with an overall grasp of the operating organization at work in an objective-oriented context. Learn to draw this flowchart of the activity in which you were involved!

You at the center of the process

Put yourself right at the center of any flowchart you may imagine – since your role is to turn inputs into outputs! Inputs coming to you for processing include raw materials, information, orders, customer complaints, and questions, among others. Processing is what you did with these inputs, such as dispatching, allocating, reporting, analyzing, conceiving, designing, etc. Outputs are the purposes of action, the outcomes; such as the quality of the service, or the solution to the problem the organization had. Remember, you are hired to solve problems!

The Flow Chart

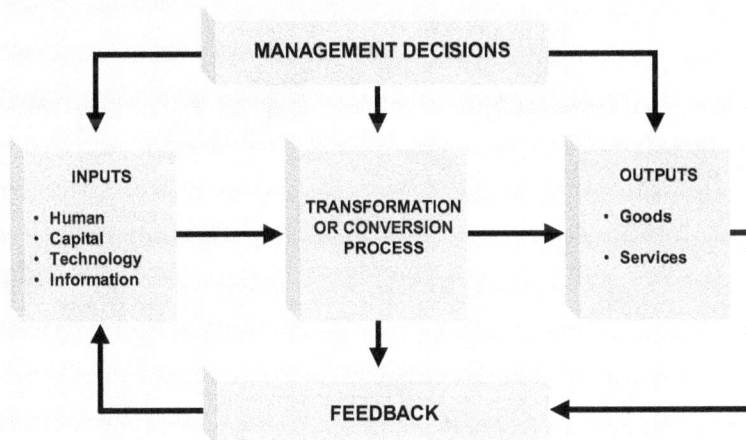

```
                    ┌─────────────────────────────┐
              ┌─────│    MANAGEMENT DECISIONS     │─────┐
              │     └─────────────────────────────┘     │
              ▼                   ▼                       ▼
        ┌──────────┐      ┌──────────────┐        ┌──────────┐
        │  INPUTS  │      │TRANSFORMATION│        │ OUTPUTS  │
        │          │ ───▶ │OR CONVERSION │ ───▶   │          │
        │ • Human  │      │   PROCESS    │        │ • Goods  │
        │ • Capital│      └──────────────┘        │          │
        │ • Technology│            │              │ • Services│
        │ • Information│           ▼              └──────────┘
        └──────────┘      ┌──────────────┐
              ▲           │   FEEDBACK   │◀──────────┘
              └───────────│              │
                          └──────────────┘
```

Learn to describe like a manager

In a CV, applicants need to learn to write both job descriptions and flowchart sentences like managers. The 'software tester' above only wrote a flowchart sentence about the major problem she dealt with. She later learned to fit that into a larger job description in which she solved other problems as well. To do this, she had to learn the concept *of job breakdown* on a CV.

On-the-job experience, like other experience you have had, will typically be laid out as in the job breakdown below. Such job breakdowns will help build a scannable, information-rich CV.

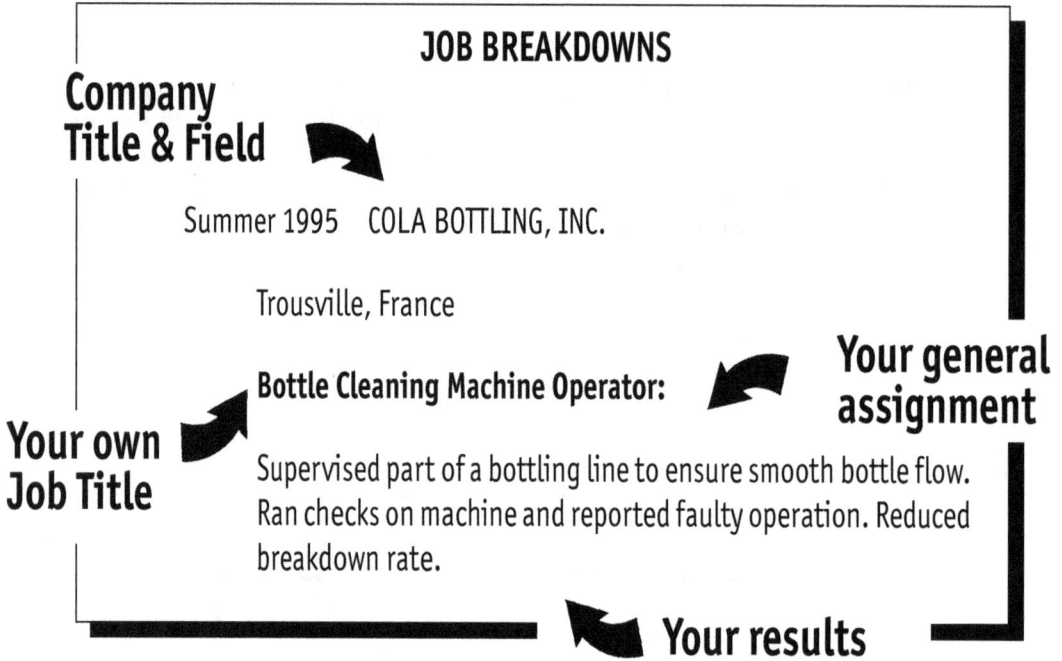

JOB BREAKDOWNS

**Company
Title & Field**

Summer 1995   COLA BOTTLING, INC.

Trousville, France

Bottle Cleaning Machine Operator:

**Your general
assignment**

**Your own
Job Title**

Supervised part of a bottling line to ensure smooth bottle flow. Ran checks on machine and reported faulty operation. Reduced breakdown rate.

Your results

JOB BREAKDOWNS

Job breakdowns do just what they say; they break an experience down into its components. In the process, the writer comes to understand the essential development he or she went through and the recruiter gains rapid insight into that development as well as into the writer's skill set.

Building a job Breakdown

Job breakdowns should include company title and area of business, your own job title, your general assignment and task; show the problems you had to solve; and conclude with outcomes.

1. Company Title

The name of the company, its field and a general address, should be laid out as follows:

Haut Buro Business Machines, Paris, France.
Sector, Economics Magazine, London, G.B.

Neither one of these companies includes in its name an explanation of its business. Therefore, the candidates had to add, either directly to the name, or as a *short explanation*, the field of industry in which the company worked. This is essential! Later in life, the first thing somebody asks you is "What are you in?" or "What do you do?" Your answer will typically start with either a job title or a business, such as: "I sell cars." This way we instantly see two levels of expertise; the person knows the car industry and he knows sales.

The next piece of information is also crucial, but may be brief: where you worked! Nobody wants to read a CV listing addresses. They want you to show yourself in a context, so a brief address of city and country will do. If they want a letter from the company, they will contact you and ask you to send them a referee's name. The location may also show you working in a foreign country and provide additional information about your skills – language and relational!

2. Job Title

Often, applicants choose a chronological CV style. Thus, they will deal with each work experience separately. In this case, they should start with a job title. This is not a 'position', but a short description in two or three words that sums up the work context for the high-speed reader.

If you have difficulty coming up with job titles to match your various jobs, internships, or extra-curricular activities, remember that a job title is **not** necessarily an official title like CEO or Vice President Marketing. These are 'positions'; a job title is rather a brief communication of your essential function in the organization. It should not be thought of as limitative, but an easy-to-read shorthand.

Often we forget that English enables us to "stack up" words in such a way that a whole sentence can be expressed in 4 words. A few years back an applicant felt that it was absolutely impossible to get across his factory job. "I was responsible for a machine that washed bottles on a line where we put wine in bottles," he said. "How do I get that in one line?"...The answer was simple:

Bottle Washing Machine Operator

This job title is probably too long. The person could have simply written:

Machine Operator

Such a job title has the advantage of being *scannable* by the high speed reader, and, as it concerns the job least related to the position the applicant is seeking right now, makes it unnecessary for the hirer to really read the job breakdown. Yet, including the words *bottle* and *washing* does allow the reader to get a very clear picture of the factory the applicant was working in.

Another common difficulty applicants encounter is expressing through a job title that they had two major functions at the same time. They feel that both should be viewable *up front*, and not hidden in the job breakdown. This calls for the combination job title.

Take the example of the applicant who had basically a secretarial job in the export orders department of a German company and wound up translating many export documents because of her linguistic skills. The German address of the company already shows that she speaks German, but she is proud of the trust the firm showed in her by asking her to translate important documents. She wrote :

Translator/Order clerk

On the following page are some 100 job titles in entry-level jobs drawn from the current business world. You should skim through them to see if any of them might help you communicate one of your past jobs.

Don't forget the excellent word 'assistant'- it can help you be accurate and honest at the same time. There's a great difference between Asst. Marketing Manager and

Marketing Manager Assistant

In the first, Asst. Marketing Manager, the person was second in rank, an experienced professional giving orders to the marketing team; whereas in the second, the person was possibly even a trainee helping the Marketing Manager for a short period, but having no rank in the hierarchy.

The job titles listed have been chosen to reflect the kinds of jobs students and young people are likely to have done as they work their way through university, do summer jobs or internships. We have avoided executive-level titles or pompous phrasing and tried to encompass a wide range of business areas. It is quite possible you will have to build your own job titles for special circumstances if you want the reader to grasp at once glance the essential of what you were doing and benefit from the scannable zoom effect described on the following pages.

Job Title List

Account assistant	Dental Assistant	Interviewer/Poller	Programmer
Accountant	Designer	Inventory clerk	Projectionist
Actuary	Die cutter	Keypunch operator	Proofreader
Administrative assistant	Disk Jockey	Lab technician	Public relations aide
Advertising Artist	Draftsman	Legal researcher	Receptionist
Advertising canvasser	Driver	Librarian	Reporter
Ambulance attendant	Editor	Life guard	Research assistant
Analyst	Electrician	Locksmith	Reservationist
Apartment Manager	Estimator	Machinist	Restaurant manager
Audio-visual assistant	Executive secretary	Mailroom clerk	Sales representative
Auditor	Exercise coach	Maintenance person/Janitor	Salesperson
Bartender	Farm laborer	Management trainee	Secretary
Billing clerk	Fashion model	Market researcher	Security guard
Bookkeeper	Fast food cook	Marketing campaign planner	Ski instructor
Bus boy	File clerk	Mechanic	Social worker
Bus driver	Flight attendant	Media analyst	Sound engineer
Buyer	Florist	Media planner	Statistician
Carpenter	Foreman	Merchandiser	Superintendent
Cartographer	Fund raiser	Messenger	Surveyor
Cashier	Furniture maker	Musician	Swimming instructor
Child care worker	Gal/guy Friday	Nurse	Switchboard operator
Computer operator	Guidance counselor	Office manager	Teacher
Copywriter	Hostess	Packager	Teller
Counselor	Hotel desk clerk	Paralegal counselor	Tool and die maker
Credit officer	Illustrator	Payroll clerk	Trader
Customer service representative	Inspector	Photographer	Translator
Data processor	Instructor	Printer	Travel agent
Decorator	Insurance agent	Product manager	Typesetter
Delivery man/girl	Interior designer	Program analyst	Underwriter
			Waiter

Now you add some of your own:

_____ _____ _____ _____

_____ _____ _____ _____

3. General Assignment/Tasks

In the first couple of sentences of the paragraph you should provide an overall view of your general responsibilities. Then you should move on to list a certain number of tasks that show the range of skills you used. The following example shows a typical job any student might have:

Personal care products merchandiser: Called on supermarkets and took orders from department managers. Conducted comparative price surveys. Organized promotional activities and managed shelf stock.

Although no particular problems are set out, we get a good look at some interpersonal and judgmental skills. This person is playing the movie that a recruiter can understand!

4. The Problem/Reaching the objective

Most often, you have dealt with an assignment that allowed you to exercise your problem-solving skills. After the job title and job assignment overview, you should focus the reader on the contribution you are most proud of. Although this might not be true of every job you have had, it has certainly occurred. At any interview you will be asked to talk about what you are most proud of – in other terms, goals you set for yourself, projects you carried through, things you have accomplished. People hire project accomplishers!

In order to successfully describe your accomplishments, you will have to relive your experiences and focus on exactly what you did that you are proud of. You have probably already done that, as you read through Chapter Three. Then, you need to depict, through a careful choice of adjectives and action verbs, the issues at stake, so that the reader can see where you are going. Above all, this is a question of structure and information. The following job breakdown by a trainee is an excellent example of an outcome-rich work experience. Some people might find it a little too long, but it shows the applicant reaching objectives. The dense detail allows the recruiter to get a good picture of her skills.

XYZ Sofa store

Saleswoman: Surveyed local sofa market to assist store manager in setting up his advertising campaign. Prepared a questionnaire and trial-tested it on 30 persons. Then polled over 180 people in the area. Analyzed the store image to improve sales strategy and reported findings to manager. Report led to revamping of store advertising campaign. Set up a price list to evaluate more accurately net margins on sales and limit excessive discounts to customers, resulting in an overall 10% increase in net margin.

5. Conclude with results/outcomes

Remember from Chapter Three how we defined results, outcomes or accomplishments. Outcomes are 'outputs' that you ensured. They are what occurred because of what you did. Yet, they are useless if we do not see what you *did* to achieve them. Outcomes must always be expressed in terms of objectives because only that way do we understand their value. Several good examples may be quoted from the saleswoman job breakdown above.

Analyzed the store image to improve sales strategy and reported findings to manager. Report led to revamping of store advertising campaign.

The objective she shows here is: to have more effective advertising in order to reach higher sales. Analyzing the store image was an intelligent action because it led to a report and thus to a revamping of the ad campaign.

The second example is clarity in management itself:

Set up a price list to evaluate more accurately net margins on sales and limit excessive discounts to customers, resulting in an overall 10% increase in net margin.

The objective is: to increase net margin and keep more of the wealth created in the store. Thus, a price breakdown was established to more accurately evaluate net margin and fine-tune discounts to increase that margin.

The communication is particularly clear-cut because *we understand why the writer did what she did.* She explained clearly the objectives of her actions, and, because of that, we see her judgment, her technical capability, and her commitment to the organization's well-being.

The above example is worth 10 jobs worked by someone who gives only one-line descriptions. In contrast, the following 'job list' shows someone who has worked a lot but we don't see the skills. The job titles are clear and tasks well described, but the job breakdowns remain superficial and hide the person's real contributions. What is missing is detail!

Lack of detail makes this list 'lifeless'

WORK EXPERIENCE

Accounting Assistant: classified papers, worked on computers, entering data about the customers

Wine store summer manager and saleswoman: Co-managed a store: assumed responsibility for summer operations.

Not enough detail!

Bank clerk: Worked at the cash desk: keyed in withdrawals and deposits.

Hostess and Organizer of yearly Theater Festival: Answered phone calls and planned the appointments of the school director.

Remember the importance of detail

Of course you cannot say everything, nor should you! Choice and order are extremely important in conveying your responsibilities and achievements. Detail plays *two* important roles in writing:

1. It creates context and clearly shows the inputs you are dealing with and the outputs you are trying to produce. So, it helps us depict skills. Choosing the right verbs, precise nouns and just enough adjectives helps make the picture three-dimensional.

2. It ensures credibility. How many of us believe the person who says "I put our group back on track"? It sounds like bragging, and possibly lying. But if the same person says – "Our group had started to come apart because of some serious differences of opinion, but nobody wanted to talk about it. So I got them together and convinced them to talk it out. Then we set up a trip together one weekend and had a lot of fun. Now we're back on track" – we tend to believe him because we see it. So detail is also ethical!

The **Zoom** Effect

The Zoom effect occurs when applicants structure a job breakdown so that it remains scannable and yet guides the reader down to the essential outcomes produced. This is done by first writing the Company Name, the Job Title, then the General Assignment and finally the special accomplishments the applicant is proud of having achieved. The following example written by a German teaching assistant in California makes this clear:

University of California, German Language Dept.
Berkeley, California

Teaching Assistant: Assigned to teach German literature conversation class for advanced students. Planned discussion sessions with Course Instructor, led weekly discussions and graded students on participation. Asked to design an experimental and challenging program for second-year students in German to increase fluency levels. Analyzed students' needs and results, tested and chose adapted teaching methods, selected texts and planned the semester schedule. Course was adopted for following year application.

She has done it all! The Zoom Effect guides the recruiter quickly through what he wants to find out: the field she worked in, the job she had, her assignment and responsibilities, finishing with her special achievements. Look at how she built the Zoom Effect on the opposite page.

The Zoom Effect

Business Field & Where ➤

University of California,
German Language Dept.

Berkeley, California

Job Title ➤

Teaching Assistant

General Assignment/ Tasks ➤

Assigned to teach German literature conversation class for advanced students. Planned discussion sessions with Course Instructor, led weekly discussions and graded students on participation.

The Problem/ Objectives ➤

Asked to design an experimental and challenging program for second-year students in German to increase fluency levels. Analyzed students' needs and results, tested and chose adapted teaching methods, selected texts and planned the semester schedule.

Outcomes Achievements ➤

Course was adopted for following year application.

WRITING THE 'FLOWCHART SENTENCE'

It takes a lot of re-thinking and structuring to write a job breakdown with its flowchart sentences. We have seen how to create the *Zoom Effect*. However, the flowchart sentence is at the heart of clear communication at scan-reading speed. Learning to write good ones will sharpen your management thinking skills.

You will learn to make all the information and materials you have dealt with *flow* towards outcomes and, thus, lead to the attainment of objectives.

The flowchart sentence's basic structure is:

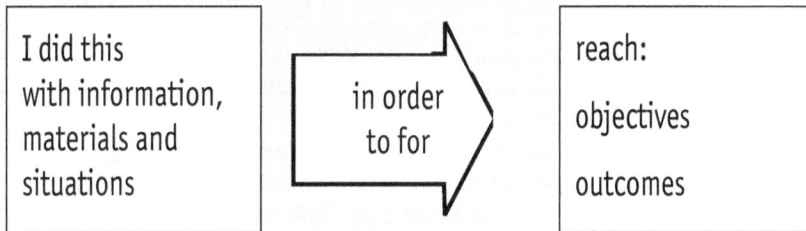

I did this with information, materials and situations	in order to for	reach: objectives outcomes

Finding the inputs and outputs

The first step in flowcharting our experience is writing it all down. By 'reliving the past' we make an inventory of all the important things we handled and did.

Reliving the past
Example 1.

Here is an example of one applicant's first attempt at reliving an important problem-solving responsibility. He has written down everything he remembered:

> *I worked for Watersystem, an aquarium-manufacturing company. Its <u>turnover dramatically plunged during summer months</u> so the company hired students to keep the sales at a reasonable level. I worked as salesman on open air markets selling a <u>new kind of cleaning system</u> people had never seen*

> *before. <u>Finding markets with open-minded and well-off people was the first task.</u> Then, I had to set my stand at places where as many people as possible would see me. The display of my stand was of utmost importance: it consisted as well in checking aquariums (taking out dead fish, dusting, choosing the right colors) <u>as making sure my stand was well located</u>. When customers were interested, <u>I had to convince them that the self-cleaning system really worked</u>. In fact that part of my job consisted in gaining their <u>confidence, confidence in the product and the company</u>, and in me as a salesman. When I sold a unit I had to talk the customer into trusting me enough, so that if he had trouble with the unit, he would bring it back and let me fix it. <u>The number of breakdowns was rather high, most of the time because of the customers themselves.</u>*

All of this was written down as it came out. Then he had to go back and 're-understand' his experience in management terms. He <u>underlined</u> the parts which seemed to be the most important. First he discovered that the objective of the company was to sell more in the 'off season' period and generally build a good image of their products. This provided him with his general assignment and the company objective. Second, he had to realize what he was 'proud of'. In this case, it was figuring out why there were so many breakdowns and gaining the trust of the public. Third, he had to remember choices he had made to carry out his assignment successfully.

He started by writing his general assignment and adding where he worked and a short, meaningful description of the product, so the reader could understand the conditions under which he had worked and the challenges he had faced in his job. He moved on to the choices he had made himself that showed he was skilled in carrying out his assignment. Then he tackled his main accomplishment and finished by showing he had reached the company's objective.

The *inputs* were the kind of system he sold, where he sold it, and the time of the year. The problem was the frequent breakdowns and the *outputs* were his success in building brand image and overcoming the breakdown problem.

This was his final version

Reaching objectives

General assignment

Salesman

- Assigned to open-air market sales of innovative aquarium cleaning systems during poor turnover period.

- Sited demonstration stand for maximum exposure to likely buyers.

Problem-solving

- Determined high breakdown rate on units sold was due to customers' misuse of system and instructed customers in correct use.

- Successfully created a quality perception of company products.

His result

Notice his use of adjectives to create context:

- <u>open-air</u> markets
- <u>innovative aquarium cleaning</u> systems
- <u>poor turnover</u> period
- <u>maximum</u> exposure
- <u>likely</u> buyers

This leaves the reader with a very clear picture of the writer's skills because he understands everything going on around him and gets a rich idea of the writer's decisions and contributions to success.

Putting the objectives and outcomes at the end

Here is another example of writing everything down before restructuring and 'weeding out' what is unimportant. In this example, the applicant has had a summer job and he is proud of what he did. Yet, it takes him some time to concretize just what he is proud of and organize it into a readable management *performance appraisal* or a simple *self-evaluation*. To do this he is going to have to put company objectives and personal outcomes at the end.

Reliving the past
Example 2.

I worked as a summer shopkeeper for Nicolini Wines in a large shopping center. I sold wines and ran the cash register. I also ordered in wines that were out of stock. I counted out the cash register every day and made the bank deposits. I worked alone except for two part-time college students. I <u>had to teach them what to do and how to serve customers</u>. I had to sweep the store and <u>reorganize the gondolas</u>. This was especially important because the shopping center was being redecorated and there was lots of noise and disturbance. <u>I was afraid customers would not buy because of these conditions. I worked hard on making it pleasant for them to look around and buy. At the end of the summer the regular shopkeeper told me I had kept the standard turnover efficiently.</u> I studied customers' tastes to be able to counsel them on the wines they wanted and did a good job selling to them because I studied wine books at night to know more about them. <u>The consumers were impressed with my knowledge.</u> The area I worked in was pretty wealthy and the wines they bought were pretty expensive.

Nicolini Wine Store

General assignment

Summer Manager: Replaced regular manager during summer vacation in upmarket shopping mall wine store. Handled all daily operations, ordered in stock, counted out register, made nightly bank deposits and trained two college students as part-time help.

Studied wine books at night to better advise customers on selections. This led to many return customers. Also frequently re-arranged store layout to overcome unpleasant shopping conditions in mall renovation period. Congratulated by manager at end of summer for maintaining sales volume in difficult conditions.

Reaching objectives

Problem-solving

Notice how this summer store manager breaks his job down into two paragraphs: the first one deals with what he considers a managerial assignment, and the second with special efforts and accomplishments he is proud of. He shows learning and willpower by recognizing the nature of his clientele, then improving his knowledge of wines and designing a store to appeal to that clientele! In writing his job breakdown, he has learned again and come to realize more about his skills. Now that he has formulated it, he will have much more to offer a future employer.

He has picked just the right verbs to *shoot a movie* of what he did. Yet, his use of adjectives is also very important:

- Upmarket shopping mall

  Shows the kind of customers he dealt with and suggests something about his relational skills and communication abilities

- Return customers

  Demonstrates that his effort in learning about wines has produced results

- Unpleasant conditions in mall renovation period

  Provides a very clear picture of the challenges he faced

- Difficult conditions

  Makes it clear how well he did!

ACTION VERBS

Choosing the right verbs for what you did

Verbs are crucial in helping us *shoot the movie* of ourselves in action. To help you understand the essential of what you did and help the recruiter to see it, we are enclosing a list of action verbs for you to draw on. Above all, they are *transitive*, i.e., they act upon things and people to produce outcomes. This book is not meant to be a dictionary, or many other verbs might be included. We have limited the list to verbs that seem to be related to management methods, functions and outcomes. To simplify things, we have grouped them according to what they show people doing:

• Dealing with information and analyzing
• Obtaining and preserving resources
• Operating or transforming
• Ensuring outcomes, making decisions
• Inventing and taking initiatives
• Working with others

Although imperfect, the list aims to help you locate verbs that best communicate what you really did and achieved. Obviously, some of the verbs could be listed in several places. At what point, for instance, does 'handled' go from just 'taking care of' something to successfully 'coping with' a problem.

Verbs dealing with information and analyzing

Analyzed	Diagnosed	Monitored
Audited	Estimated	Recorded
Balanced	Examined	Researched
Checked	Identified	Reviewed
Consulted	Indexed	Studied
Controlled	Interviewed	Surveyed
Costed	Investigated	Verified
Detected	Logged	

© Éditions d'Organisation

Verbs dealing with obtaining and preserving resources

Acquired	Gathered	Received
Assembled	Hired	Recruited
Bought	Maintained	Secured
Collected	Obtained	Selected
Compiled	Protected	Tested
Conserved	Purchased	

Verbs dealing with operating and transforming, having to do with 'roles' or 'functions'

Administered	Dispensed	Organized
Advised	Distributed	Oversaw
Arbitrated	Drafted	Performed
Automated	Drew up	Planned
Budgeted	Edited	Prepared
Calculated	Filed	Prescribed
Catalogued	Formulated	Presided
Charted	Guided	Processed
Classified	Handled	Promoted
Closed	Headed	Provided
Compounded	Implemented	Referred
Computed	Inspected	Routed
Conducted	Installed	Scheduled
Contacted	Lectured	Served
Converted	Marketed	Served as
Converted	Mediated	Sold
Coordinated	Negotiated	Supplied
Corresponded	Opened	Trained

Counseled	Operated	Translated
Critiqued	Ordered	Wrote

Verbs with ensuring outcomes, decisions, 'deliveries'

Accounted for	Eliminated	Procured
Achieved	Enhanced	Produced
Arranged	Enlarged	Realized
Ascertained	Ensured	Reduced
Assessed	Exceeded	Reported
Attained	Expanded	Restored
Awarded	Facilitated	Retained
Built	Followed up	Scheduled
Carried out	Founded	Strengthened
Completed	Generated	Structured
Consolidated	Improved	Synthesized
Constructed	Increased	Trimmed
Delivered	Interpreted	Updated
Demonstrated	Packaged	Upgraded
Designed	Presented	Was awarded
Determined	Prevented	Worked out
Developed		Wrote up

Verbs showing inventiveness, initiative and leadership

Adapted	Encouraged	Proposed
Approved	Engineered	Recommended
Attained	Established	Refined
Awarded (was)	Facilitated	Reorganized
Brought about	Forecasted	Repositioned

Clarified	Initiated	Revamped
Conceived	Integrated	Revised
Congratulated (was)	Introduced	Set up
Coped with	Invented	Solved
Created	Located	Spearheaded
Criticized	Mastered	Streamlined
Decided	Overcame	Succeeded
Devised	Overhauled	Systematized
Differentiated	Perfected	Turned around
Discovered	Persuaded	Undertook
Disproved	Piloted	

Verbs dealing with working with people

Assisted	Explained	Seconded
Coached	Instructed	Served as
Communicated	Participated	Supervised
Directed	Represented	Taught

Verbs which are not action verbs

There are many verbs which are not included, but some have been intentionally avoided because we feel they are not action verbs but empty verbs which only throw up a smoke screen and cloud over what you were really doing. These verbs should definitely be *struck out* because they mean everything and nothing! They are:

~~Managed~~ & ~~Motivated~~

There may be others, but over the years we have found that people use them when they don't know how to say what they want to say. Managing is your job, and you will still have to say what you did in order to manage. Motivating will lead someone to ask you how you did it, and so you might as well explain precisely at the outset.

APPLYING THE JOB BREAKDOWN STYLE TO NON-JOB ACHIEVEMENTS

Before we move on to Chapter Five and discuss how to structure the CV for your specific situation, we should remember that accomplishments and learning come from many things we have done, and not just paid work situations. As we pointed out in Chapter Three, results also come from extra-curricular activities, volunteer work, hobbies, home activities and travel. If you are proud of what you have done in such activities and feel they say something important about you, the exact same five-step method developed for work experience may be used for these off-the-job activities. This is particularly important for students looking for internships or jobs when they have never worked before. We all have life experiences and they teach us just as much as work. They have built our skills and their lessons may be carried over to work assignments. Let's see how the five-step method applies to non-professional experience:

1	Company Name	This time it may turn out to be a sports club or other non-profit organization, but it provides context just as in the case of companies and their fields.
2	Job Title	Once again, it provides a scannable view of main assignment.
3	General Assignment	The assignment may be self-assigned but it outlines the main things you were taking care of.
4	Objectives/problem	Shows what you focused on and reveals skills and learning.
5	Outcomes	No less real for performance assessment than paid work experience.

On the next page, we have included a small number of true examples out of context to show how the job breakdown method fits perfectly with these 'outside' activities.

EXAMPLES OF STUDENT ACHIEVEMENTS USING THE JOB BREAKDOWN STYLE

- Collected donations in the school fundraising drive from various corporations, contacted management, phone-canvassed for donators. Helped raise 20% more than previous year.

- **Sailing Instructor:** Taught sailing in the biggest sailing school in Europe, the Club XYZ, as specialist of catamarans and centerboarder regattas. Instructed trainees on advanced techniques of sailing and racing. Planned training course and evaluated difficulties and learners' progress. Completed catamarans special tuning.

- **Reporter** for the School "Today's Business Leaders" Club. Participated in a reporting project to write articles on management for the French press. Coordinated a 20-person team interviewing Paris business leaders. Co-drafted questionnaires and interviewed several leaders. Collated and analyzed the results. Co-authored an extensive report published in a major French business magazine.

- Produced the "Misunderstanding" by French playwright Albert Camus, organized and promoted the amateur theatre company tour: designed and printed posters, advertised on local radio stations.

APPLYING THE JOB BREAKDOWN STYLE TO CURRENT ACTIVITIES

When writing your CV, you will rightfully point out that not everything is *past*. You are probably doing something right now that you would like to talk about in your CV. If so, nothing really changes, except that you will use the same kinds of action verbs in the simple present for your general assignment and tasks.

> Ensure quality customer service. Follow up all customer complaints.

However, if you want to stress one particular project you are carrying through at the time and for which you want to show particular involvement, you will use the present continuous, for instance:

> Currently training two recent recruits in customer service techniques.

PRACTICE EXERCISES

On the following pages, before going on to the chapter on structuring a CV, we encourage you to practice reliving your most meaningful on – and off-the-job experiences, as did the applicants on the previous pages. We have provided some forms for you to work on. Work on **every** experience!

One warning! Remember that we always understand ourselves. However, others may not. After you relive your experience and turn it into a job breakdown, *bounce it off* your friends to find out if they can *visualize* the experience, the problems, the skills and the outcomes the way you want them to. Talk it over with them until you find the words that get your *movie* across! Trying it out on critical-minded friends is essential to make sure of the clarity of your communication.

Your practice sheets

General assignment

Main tasks carried out under this assignment:

_____

_____

_____

_____

_____

The objectives involved in this assignment were to:

_____

_____

_____

_____

How did these objectives fit into the department or company objectives (or organizational objectives – club, etc.)?

_____

_____

_____

_____

My special assignment or problem to solve

Clear description of the purpose of carrying out the special assignment

_____

_____

_____

List the 'raw materials' and 'tools' used

_____

_____

Outcomes

What was improved, accomplished, etc.

_____

_____

_____

_____

_____

_____

_____

_____

Now write your final job breakdowns

_____

_____

_____

_____

_____

_____

_____

_____

_____

_____

_____

_____

_____

_____

_____

_____

Key points in chapter four

- When you write your CV you are sitting an interview.

- Understand what the interviewer wants to learn about you with his questions.

- Write your own interview questions.

- Write detailed answers to your own interview questions.

- Make your CV into a 'movie' that shows you using skills to solve problems.

- Learn to break down all your past experience to show why you were doing what you were doing and how you were doing it.

- Souvenez-vous : quand vous rédigez votre CV, vous passez votre premier entretien.

- Comprenez bien ce que le recruteur cherchera à savoir sur vous par le biais des questions qu'il vous posera.

- N'hésitez pas à imaginer et écrire ces questions.

- Répondez à ces questions par écrit et de manière détaillée.

- Construisez votre CV comme s'il s'agissait d'un film qui montre la façon dont vous résolvez les problèmes en utilisant vos compétences.

- Efforcez-vous de décomposer vos expériences profession-nelles passées afin de bien montrer ce que vous avez fait, comment vous l'avez fait, pourquoi vous l'avez fait.

146

- Find a job title for each one of your jobs that explains what you did.

- Always show the results of what you did.

- Give good detail so the recruiter can really see you working.

- Use the Zoom effect.

- Find the right action verbs to describe what you contributed.

- Remember that the job breakdown approach can be used with any non-job accomplishment.

- Pour chaque expérience passée trouvez un titre qui résume de manière explicite ce que vous avez fait.

- Montrez toujours les résultats de ce que vous avez fait.

- Donnez suffisamment de détails pour que le recruteur puisse vous imaginer au travail.

- Utilisez l'effet de "zoom".

- Un verbe d'action bien choisi montrera très bien votre contribution passée.

- Souvenez-vous que ce découpage des actions passées peut-être utilisé pour n'importe quelle réalisation que vous mentionnez dans le CV.

How to structure the CV

Now that you have carried through a complete inventory of your skills and personal qualities as well as learned to write short documentary '*movies*' of your accomplishments, you are ready to put it all together into a CV that suits your particular situation and the kind of job you are looking for!

We will review the *four* different types of CVs that may be used, as well as their advantages and drawbacks. Just remember that *there is no conventional, right structure for a CV*; there is only the CV that the reader finds easy to understand and that paints a picture of yourself clearly, quickly and accurately.

Nevertheless, whatever structure you use, there are certain *subjects* that all recruiters will expect to see you talk about, because it is on the information you provide under these headings that they will base their decision to call you to an interview or not.

BASIC INFORMATION TO PROVIDE ON ANY CV

Experience and Education are the two most important parts of any CV. All your capabilities and skills to perform useful services for the company should normally be visible through these headings. However, in Europe, languages are often separated out as an individual heading, since the mastery of 'foreign' languages is so crucial for doing business in Europe and in the World. A section devoted to things that seem more specific about the applicant is often included and may be labeled *Personal, Special Interests,* and so on. I encourage applicants to create another heading which I call *Achievements or Accomplishments* to include other things you are proud of that do not seem to fit anywhere else.

Actually, you have a great freedom to *label* these subjects as you wish, to *choose the order* in which you talk about them and to decide what you include under them. Languages, for instance, could be talked about separately, included under Education, Experience or possibly Personal – perhaps you were raised in Germany in Spanish by your parents! Remember simply to use *few* headings and to organize the information under them in a way that the reader understands where you want to go!

Education

Writing about your education usually poses two problems: 1) Do I put *Education* first or second? 2) How do I make somebody in another country understand my degrees? The answer to the first question is fairly simple, whereas the second can seem quite complex in a Europe with so many different educational programs and degrees.

Do I put Education first or last or somewhere else ?

Put your Education first:

• When you feel your education says the most about the skills you are trying to sell! This is typically true when you have just graduated and are looking for your first full-time job.

• When you have made a career change, been re-trained for a new profession and feel that your experience does not permit you to focus on enough job-related skills.

Put your Education second:

• When your experience shows more about your skills than your education does

• When years of work experience separate you from your school or university years.

How do I talk about my degrees ?

"My degrees are German. I have a 'Vordiplom'. How is the recruiter in France going to understand that?"

"I graduated from a French IUT in 'Action Commerciale'. How is an English company going to understand what I have studied?"

"I am finishing my 5th year in a Spanish University. How do I explain the level of education to a recruiter in Poland?"

"I hold a degree from a Business School in Sweden. In Milan, will they understand how well I have been trained?"

These questions are becoming more and more common as young people aim at jobs *crossborder* and realize that there are apparently great differences in educational systems around Europe. They are afraid that they will not stand a chance in competing with a native of the country they are writing to, because their degrees and school systems are different!

You may very well be in this situation. In many ways, it may be to your advantage! Remember the following points:

• You are sending a CV in English. This is already positive because it shows you think internationally rather than domestically.

• You are applying for a job outside your own country or for a job with an international company and international opportunities. You are showing you are ready for those opportunities.

• Your target company's working language may not be your native tongue, nor even the language of the country in which they are based.

• Recruiters are quite aware that many differences exist among educational systems; they are more interested in a level of education and a *content* of education than details about the system in your country! Explaining your country's educational system is <u>not</u> the answer!

Most countries have both university systems and secondary or advanced vocational training schools. Some countries have preparatory schools, like France, which prepares secondary schools graduates for France's *Grandes Ecoles*' competitive entrance examinations. Other countries do not, except Japan. In the US, on the other hand, the intellectual abilities of students in their last year of secondary school is assessed by nationally administered aptitude tests. Some universities have four year programs, others five. The variety of systems is endless!

The importance of the number of years of study

Almost everyone recognizes the Anglo-Saxon degrees: Bachelor's, Masters and Ph.D., or Doctorate. The M.Sc. or Master's of Science one year specialization degree is also becoming widely known. The Bachelor's is recognized as being equivalent in Europe to three years of university studies and is considered the end of *undergraduate studies*. Any degree awarded for two or three years of study in Europe would usually be considered an undergraduate degree. In the US, a Bachelor's usually takes four years. In Europe, when you are in your fourth year of university studies, or more, you would usually be considered in "postgraduate" studies.

Doctorate Ph. D.	Postgraduate research degree
M. Sc., M.B.A. Postgraduate specialization	5 to 6 years of university
Master's	4 to 5 years of university
Bachelor's	3 years of university
Undergraduate degrees	2 years of higher education
Secondary education High School	

Two year programs and shorter

Many countries have two year undergraduate programs which serve as pre-requisites to moving on to the Bachelor's and Master's levels. This is true of the French two-year DEUG and the German *Vordiplom*. Other two year programs focus on practical vocational training. These courses may be taught in Secondary Educational Institutions, University Institutes or private school, and are considered more operational programs rather than conceptual programs. All of these may be referred to as an "Undergraduate Degree in...., X School or X University."

Short duration specialization programs might be called Certificate programs if they do not lead to what is commonly referred to as a diploma.

Postgraduate studies

Postgraduate programs after the Master's level, usually occurring in the fifth or sixth year of study, are becoming more common everywhere. In these programs, both recent graduates, and professionals changing careers, seek a more-focused, higher-level, one-year specialization in fields such as Human Resource Management, Plant Management or Bank Management, among others. These may be referred to as "Postgraduate degree in ...", or "M.Sc. [Master in Science] equivalent in..." Admission to these programs typically requires a Master's equivalent degree, but often work experience is accepted instead. This only shows that what is being assessed is a level of professional maturity and learning that may not necessarily be acquired in school!

When you are in doubt about how to explain your degrees, adding the word 'equivalent' after the degree clearly shows its level and also tells the truth! Look at this list of examples:

4 to 5 years of study

June 1997	Vordiplom, undergraduate degree, University of Bayreuth, Germany. Specialized in Business and Economics.
June 1999	Master's in Engineering equivalent, Catholic Electronics Institute, Lyon, France
Sept-Dec 98	Certificate Program in Export. Paris Chamber of Commerce.

Two years of German university

Specialization of brief duration

The word 'graduation' in English is used at many levels, but above all, for finishing one's basic higher educational studies. In some cases, you might simply point out that you have 'graduated' from a certain school, as did these two applicants:

Sept. 1999	Graduated from the Lausanne School of Hotel Management and Tourism.
Sept. 1999	Graduated from ESJ School of Journalism, Lille, France. Majored in Audio-visual communications.

The number of years of study can help the European recruiter situate your intellectual maturity and overcome difficulties in communicating degree equivalents. Take the following example of a Swedish girl seeking an internship, who has not yet graduated:

1998-99	One year exchange studies at X Graduate School of Management, Nice, France. Following courses in French.
1996-2000	Göteburg Business School, Sweden. Majoring in Marketing
1994-1995	French Studies, University of Stockholm, Sweden
1994	Graduated from Calabasas High School, California, USA.
1993	Graduated from Stockholm High School

Reading in 1999, the recruiter can see right away that the internship applicant has finished four years of university and will graduate with a Master's equivalent. He can also see her international experience. Although the High School graduation is not really important, because it was followed by university studies, it *does* give an idea of the applicant's age and the number of years of studies following. Schools in different countries should always be included because of the international character they lend to your portrait and the information they provide on your language skills.

Avoid problems in labeling degrees

Serious problems may arise in countries where too many different degrees exist and there is a tendency to use abbreviations: DEA, CAAE, MSG, CLC, ICA, etc. Most of these should not be used, nor even translated. They should even be *spelled out* on your native language CV, because domestic recruiters may not understand them. Imagine the reaction of a non-French recruiter who reads in the following French girl's CV:

June 1999	CAAE, IAE, Lyon, France
June 1996	CLC, Sorbonne, Paris, France

The reader hasn't got the slightest idea of what she has studied. She is talking only to herself! On the other hand, if she had simply written as below, the recruiter would have a clear idea of her education:

June 1999	Postgraduate degree in Management, IAE, Business Administration Institute, Lyon, France
June 1996	Bachelor's equivalent in Classical Arabic, Sorbonne University, Paris, France

Notice how she has kept IAE, but she has also added an explanation – 'Business Administration Institute' – as if it were part of its name. This ensures that any mail sent to the IAE Business Administration Institute will reach its destination, and yet, the recruiter will understand what kind of school it is.

Many schools in Europe have already created their English identity for international communication purposes. Contact your school or university to find out what their official title in English is. Also find out if they have chosen an English-language equivalent of their degrees. If not, it is generally a good idea to give your degrees in your native language and put English equivalents next to them.

The idea of 'Majors'

The English idea of 'majors' or specializations in education is very useful to add after your degree if you wish to show that you have a more in-depth knowledge of some field. If you have graduated already, you may add, for instance, "Majored in Finance", or, if you are still in university, "Majoring in Finance". Brief information on the curriculum might be useful, as in the following example.

1996-2000	Business and Economics, University of Mannheim, Germany. Majoring in International Management. Focus on French language and culture.

A long list of courses will seldom be read and steals space from more useful information. It is up to you to think about those parts of your university program that should be stressed. In the example above, in three short lines, the student has shown the general business education he is getting, his more advanced understanding of international management, and his suitability to work in a French-related context.

Work Experience

You have spent a great deal of time in Chapters Three and Four analyzing your skills on the job and learning to write job breakdowns. So you are quite ready to write the *Work Experience* part of your CV! However, European applicants often see a difference between jobs worked to earn extra money from internships or traineeships that are performed as part of a university or degree requirement.

158

Internships or jobs?

Recent graduates are often more proud of the internships they have performed as part of their studies than the jobs they held to make a living! Except that internships may not be paid, there is no real difference from the experience point of view. This should be clear from Chapter Four. Therefore, all of them may be included under *Work Experience*. If some provided greater scope for your talents and development, then you only have to decide whether to talk about *all of them* or not.

Working in a butcher store is perfectly honest and useful work; on the other hand, the internship you performed carrying out a market survey may show more of the skills you are trying to convey. If you have worked a lot, do not try to put everything. Trying to include everything may produce a long and tiring CV, 'undigested' for the reader.

In some countries, students do very little paid work during their studies, because the habits of the economy do not make it feasible, or studies are very time-consuming. In other countries, however, students are used to finding part-time jobs after school and during the summer. Internships are not a very developed part of the education in Anglo-Saxon countries, although part-time work is. In Finland and Sweden, many students will work part time to help make ends meet. In Germany and France, internships are a key part of the *professional school* education system, but a little less in the university system. In Italy, Spain, and Portugal internships are becoming more frequent, but many students at the Master's level will only have one 'work' experience.

Whatever your situation, experience of work is very important to talk about in a CV. If you have very little work experience, look for non-job accomplishments and achievements to sell your skills. They often provide training every bit as good as on-the-job training!

Languages

It goes without saying that the "Languages" heading is extremely important on CVs where applicants are offering skills to work internationally. Unfortunately, they are often presented very routinely and not very convincingly, so they become the most *boring* part of the CV. The style below is typical:

LANGUAGES

Swedish:	mother tongue
English:	fluent
French:	excellent command
Italian:	good command

After all, what you are selling is *skills*. A good question might be "What can you do in these languages?" Can you play – or can you work? Are they language skills for traveling and getting around, or are they for negotiating contracts, working with company staff and dealing with customers on the phone? Think of them in terms of performance skills. If you have studied in a foreign university, mentioning it under Languages might be a good idea. Special language awards, language diplomas, and stays abroad are more impressive than a one-week tour of the country. Let's see what the above applicant might do if she were our Swedish girl from Göteburg on the previous pages:

LANGUAGES

Swedish: **Mother tongue**

English: **Fluent.** One year of study in an American High School. 90% of university reading in English-language textbooks. Many lectures in English in Sweden.

French: **Excellent command.** Now studying in French Business School, following all courses and writing reports in French.

Italian: **Good command.** Many pleasure trips to Italy. Understand TV and radio. Can write simple letters.

Other mentions might be made of Chamber of Commerce Diplomas in a language, the Cambridge and TOEFL scores in English, etc. One of the best recommendations of your skill in English is, of course, writing a *good* CV in English. *One warning:* in an English CV, never forget to sell your own native language!

Accomplishments or Achievements

Accomplishments, achievements or results you are proud of have been developed in Chapter Three. When you have drawn up a list of accomplishments, you may find that they cannot easily be classified under Work Experience. Perhaps they come from activities that are not work-related. If you create an Accomplishments or Achievements heading, using the job breakdown method, this heading can be a very positive on a CV! In some cases, these experiences may sell management and organizational skills far better than what you have written under Work Experience. They may also be more entrepreneurial, having required volunteer effort. Remember, however, that if you were a 'member' of a group, this is not an achievement; you must show what you *did* as a member!

Where do I put the rest?

This is a problem! You have other things you want to say about yourself and you don't know how to classify them. *If they are useful at all*, they might be organized under *Special Interests, Special Activities, Interests and Activities, Skills and – Personal.* We suggest you avoid a special heading for Leisure Activities and Sports, which, if they contain many entries, seem to suggest you are only interested in leisure and sports.

If you use one of the above headings, make sure it expresses well what follows. To list computer software skills under *Special Activities* has no sense. To list your driving license under Special Interests is equally meaningless. In any case, talking about your driving license on an international CV is silly, unless you want to drive a truck, for instance!

DON'T SHOW TRASH IN YOUR CV!

Avoid using your last heading on the CV as a kind of 'catch-all' or trash can. If it is a *trash can*, do not show what is in it! Avoid the word *Miscellaneous*, which means that everything under this heading is really not necessary. Remember that everything on a CV should be absolutely necessary!

What constitutes really useful information beyond the four headings of Education, Work Experience, Languages and Accomplishments we have already discussed? The answer is: not much! There are some exceptions:

- If you know how to use different software packages and Internet, that often deserves its own heading: *Computer Skills* with examples of accomplishments included, unless you have already put some major piece of work you have done under the *Accomplishments* heading.

COMPUTER SKILLS

Microsoft Office, Desktop Publishing: Pagemaker, Photoshop. Research project for our Marketing Department carried out on Internet.

- Sports activities need no detail unless they are related to major perseverance skills, organization of events or community service. *Teaching* sports to others is a very positive entry. This stresses patience, entrepreneurship and communication skills. Once again, in this case, this might come better under *Accomplishments*.

Consider these examples of computer skills and sports developed under Accomplishments:

ACCOMPLISHMENTS

- Set up at data base to follow up the graduates from our Engineering School. Designed base and ran a team of volunteers to key in data.

- Founded a sailing association. Organized and conducted training meetings.

- Taught soccer on weekends to children from underprivileged urban areas. Organized matches between different towns.

Movie-going, reading, piano and the like are relatively useless, but you may feel like *fleshing out* the portrait of yourself at the end of the CV. In this case *Personal Interests* is a fine heading and simply listing the three interests will suffice. It is not really clear what it says about you that will help the recruiter, but it does perhaps humanize a little.

PERSONAL INTERESTS: Movie-going, reading, piano

OK, but not really important!

WHAT INFORMATION SHOULD YOU GIVE UP?

We have already pointed out that a lot of personal data about your hobbies, sports and leisure activities might not be as important as adding one more line about your real achievements or a well-developed job breakdown that shows your job skills. Other information can also be simplified. One example is your address.

Addresses

Applicants often have two addresses, particularly if they are studying: their weekend address and the school week address. *Put only one address on a CV, the one where you want to get important mail.* Two addresses is asking the recruiter to send two letters or make two phone calls – and they 'trash up' your CV! It is up to you to make yourself easy to find. If you put e-mail, read it often! Some people put their e-mail address because it shows they are modern and Internetted, but they actually use it very little. Since companies use it more and more, they count on you reading your e-mail, although they will probably send you normal mail to call you for an interview.

Your age

Should you put your age or not? This is a big debate. The answer may vary from country to country. One thing is sure: you can seem too young for a job and you can seem too old for a job! We have seen the example of a girl seeking an internship in financial products who wrote a brilliant letter but mentioned that she was nineteen right in the middle of the letter. All her classmates were 22 or older. She didn't get the internship, possibly because she seemed too young for that service. She didn't really need to give her age, because her education second on the CV would have shown that she was probably in her early 20s, like most people finishing their Bachelor's level.

When it comes to *Career Starters*, their age is probably not a negative point, but probably not positive either. On the other hand, *Career Changers* might range from mid-20s to their late 40s, and beyond. In these cases, age could become a positive or very negative factor. If you are not sure whether it is positive or negative, do not put it on the CV. Sell your skills and background, get to the interview and let them ask you your age there. Often job offerings in the press specify an age range, such as 30 to 35. If you are 38, are you going to refuse to apply, because you are outside the range? Of course not, you are going to sell your skills, and at the interview the recruiter is going to decide that the age criteria was not the most important thing.

Older applicants in a time of high unemployment have no particular reason to put their age up front as opposed to other important information about themselves. Younger applicants often feel that being young is positive, because they bring in new ideas and 'dynamism'. Recruiters could just as easily consider them 'green' or inexperienced. Dynamism is also very hard to define. In a letter, dynamism can only be sold if there are concrete references to your accomplishments linked to what you call dynamism.

Age or birthday?

For those of you who do decide your age is a serious enough plus to put on the CV, just type it as "25 years old." Do not put birthdays or birthplaces. Some people feel this is interesting information. It is true that occasional recruiters want to know your Zodiac sign and feel this tells them something important about you. But what if they do not like your Zodiac sign? They can get this kind of information when you fill out the company forms or Internet applications anyway, but on a CV the fact you were born on March 13th or November 12th is of no interest and less easy to understand than "25 years old."

Birthplace?

Once again, only if it is interesting. If you were born in New York or Hong Kong, this might seem an interesting point for a European recruiter – perhaps not! New York might suggest you are fluent in English, although you left at the age of one. Hong Kong might suggest the same thing, or it might suggest you are Chinese. Most birthplaces offer little useful information you can control.

Nationality

This is a piece of information all of us should be proud of and it may provide useful information to a cross-border hirer. If you feel that your nationality, for some reason, will <u>not</u> be a plus in getting you to the interview, then do not include it. Even Nokia's on-line application form does not ask for it. Of course, your address may suggest nationality, and everybody is interested in your language skills. Your nationality may also suggest knowledge of certain ways of working which is almost certainly useful to the company.

Mistakes to avoid......

In summary, common mistakes to avoid are:

- **Talking to yourself:** using abbreviations or jargon from a company that cannot be understood by others. If you belong to an organization or have won a prize, spell out the name and purpose of the organization and the reason for the prize. If you are a student and want to show you have been a serious one, do not use your marks or grade point average. A 1.8 in Germany might be 16 in France. Some countries grade more generously than others, some schools too. Give rather your ranking in the school, i.e., "top 15% of graduating class."

- **Touching on sensitive areas:** avoid mentioning politics and religion. If you have good experience in organizing or assisting in political campaigns and feel it needs to be mentioned, keep it general and don't give the party or candidate name.

- **Trying to say everything:** Learn to put only what is most important. Remember the one page rule and that the recruiter would prefer to read meaningful and informative sections about yourself than a list of dates and events.

- **Organizing badly:** Be careful in choosing your headings and what to put under them. Check that everyone understands why some information is under a certain heading.

- **Providing irrelevant or negative information:** This is sometimes difficult to judge. Should you talk about wives, husbands, children, divorces, birth dates, birth places, etc? Our attitude is that it has nothing really to do with your offer of professional and human skills. It is also difficult to control the reader's reaction to this information. One of our seminar participants in the past *started* her CV with:

Divorced, two dependant children	←	**This on a CV?**

When we asked her why she did this, her answer was "Because it's true!" Nevertheless, it constituted a *triple* mistake: first, putting it at the top of the CV put off the recruiter, who was looking for information about her *skills*; second, it made it seem as though she was asking for help, rather than offering it; third, it may have provided negative information, suggesting to *some* that she would be too busy raising her children to work!

You may answer: "It's none of the recruiter's business." Then, if it isn't, don't talk about it – talk only business! Such subjects may come up at the interview, but that's a better place to deal with them. First, let's get to the interview!

CREATE A PERSONALIZED STRUCTURE THAT SUITS BOTH YOUR SPECIAL CASE AND THE JOB !

Almost every untrained CV-writer will automatically write his or her CV as a chronological *list* of degrees and jobs. The writer will assume 'that this is the way it is done!' He or she will avoid taking any risks, breaking any rules and be afraid of shocking the reader – without thinking about what contribution the organization of information makes to the CV. Actually there are *four* basic structures that may be used, and even *mixed* successfully:

1. The Chronological CV
2. The Skills or Experience Areas CV
3. The Abilities and Achievements CV
4. The Letter/CV Combination

Chronological

JACQUES DRISCOLL
96, Ave de Neuilly
75019 Paris
France

WORK EXPERIENCE
1995-Present   DIGITAL ELECTONIX
               Paris, France.

               General Sales Manager: Started as Regional Sales Manager for Southern France. Brought in as General Sales Manager to develop and implement strategies to increase sales to corporate clients in worsening economic climate. Reported directly to CEO. Turned around performance of undermotivated sales management team by redesigning compensation packages and reallocating sales areas in line with sales representatives' profiles. Personally followed major national accounts and strengthened company's position as sole supplier. Sales performance increased by 27%.

1992-1995   PRESSE DIFFUSION
               Grenoble, France

               District Sales Manager: Worked directly with five magazine wholesalers and dozens of retail accounts to increase circulation of publications. Overcame resistance to innovative publications and gained considerable exposure for breakthrough specialized magazines for the younger set. Added 30% new and profitable accounts to company's line.

1988-1992   DIVERSIFIED PRODUCTS, INC
               Hong Kong

               Independent Product/Market Representative: Conducted market studies and consulted with sporting goods distributors and retailers of to determine potential demand for Diversified's executive exercise equipment. Concluded existing distribution circuits were ill-adapted to Diversified's specificity and developed contacts with multinational businesses' headquarters to outfit in-house executive health spas. Successfully placed company products with over 100 corporations and ensured after sales service. Left a permanent sales structure.

LANGUAGES
               French: mother tongue. English: fluent, four years English selling experience in Honk Kong.

EDUCATION
1987   Master's in Economics and Business, Catholic University of Lille, France.

Skills or Experience Areas

Dieter Schneider
Address

Job Objective: **Financial analyst for Corporate Loans Department of a Bank**

FINANCE EXPERIENCE
• Currently completing a Master's at FHU Graduate School of Management, Frankfurt, Germany, with a **specialization in Finance.**
• Performed pre-acquisition financial analysis in the **Mergers & Acquisitions** Department, Nikko Bank, Germany. Assigned to Services Acquisitions Team. Wrote up detailed reports on target companies for Services Acquisition Manager. Dec - Feb 1999
• **Assisted Comptroller** of HSSA IT Services, Aachen, Germany in redesigning system to follow outstanding accounts. June - Aug 1998
• **Accounting internship** for Motorenwerke Motors; Stuttgart, Germany. Handled computerized ledger entries. July & Aug 1996

INTERNATIONAL EXPERIENCE
German and American nationality
Working abroad
Ceros, Ltd., Sheffield, **Great Britain.** Marketing Department. Carried out demand and competitor analysis on major EU photocopier markets. Wrote report on recommendations and presented it to Management Committee. May - Aug 1999
Education abroad
• MBA studies at Notre Dame University, South Dakota, **USA.** Sept - Dec 1999
• Economics and Business, University of Montpellier, **France.** Feb - June 1999
• Exchange program at Harvard Military Academy, Los Angeles, California, USA. 1994-1996
• Participation in student exchange programs in high schools in **UK** and **France** through my German High School.
Languages
German: native language. English: fluent. French: good command.

KNOWLEDGE OF DIFFERENT BUSINESSES
First-hand experience of Banking, IT Services, Industrial Machinery and Motors, Hotel and Resorts, Photocopiers and Digital Office Automation.

Abilities & Achievements

JAMES MANN
2569 Arunda Heights ,Purley
SURREY CR22HF
England

Job Target: **Project Manager for Financial Services Marketing**

ABILITIES
• advising marketing managers on communication approaches to adopt in advertising in English-speaking countries.
• providing professional English-writing services to continental corporations wishing to market their products worldwide.
• full design start to finish of advertising brochures for corporations and universities for overseas.
• writing and recording of professional sales films.
• setting up schedules, performance measurement methods and reporting procedures for team members and debriefing effectively.
• communicating a high level of ideas on financial products and capital markets to demanding publics and leading effective financial negotiations.

ACHIEVEMENTS
• completely conceived and wrote 120 page bulletin for English Graduate School for its overseas marketing purposes.
• wrote scripts and recorded films for major French and Belgian corporations' marketing services.
• translated major French economic treatise on EC for American market.
• planned, organized, and directed management curriculum at major business schools and universities.
• produced schematics, feasibility studies, reports and cost estimates.
• drafted successful bid for EU funding for major educational technology transfer to Eastern Europe.
• managed technology transfer project, including selection of teachers, supervision of course content, payment of all services, and contacts with European partners.
• wrote case studies in organizational design and finance for management education and ran seminars on financial analysis and negotiation.

WORK HISTORY
1985-Present - Associate Professor, International Affairs Dept., Southland University, England
1980-1983 -Instructor of History, UCLA

EDUCATION
1985 - Postgraduate degree in Management, Lille University, France
1983 - Ph.D./ABD, History, UCLA
1974, 78 - B.A., M.A., History, UCLA

Letter/CV Combination

157 Avenue Jan Rays
Rotterdam, Netherlands
October 20, 1999

Mr. Alfred Simpson
CF Consultants
66 Wood Lane, Hempstead
Hertfordshire HP2 4RG
England

Dear Mr. Simpson :

I believe with my wide experience in financial management and counseling, dealing with budgets, planning, forecasting and problem solving I could make a serious contribution to your firm's consulting tasks. Some of my recent achievements are:

Provided financial strategic planning for a large banking institution through careful scanning of the regulatory environment and governmental policy changes. Sold off high-risk assets, reduced off balance sheet items and created innovative financing package to help bank meet new capital adequacy requirements within three years.

Advised corporate clients on prospective acquisitions by thorough analysis of holdings portfolios and past and projected cash flows of target companies. Provided financial engineering services for buyers on both capital and debt markets and assisted clients in non-core business asset sales to quickly reduce debt burden and guarantee acquisitions' viability.

Recruited over 20 finance and economics professionals for banking and corporate clients nearly all of whom moved into senior management positions.

Conducted management seminars on the interpretation of economic and monetary conditions, forecasting models and the use of such data in decision-making.

I hold a Master's in Economics, an International MBA from Tredint University and a Ph.D. degree from IMA.

I would like to meet with you and discuss my future contributions to your firm. I will call you in a week or so.

Sincerely,

G van Tafeel

Gert van Tafeel
32.56.20.10.61

Any of these structures may be used whether you are seeking a full-time job or just applying for an internship period. There is no real difference in the way you write the *content* of your CV – you are always trying to convince the hirer you will be useful on the job, whether for two months or years to come!

Remember as well that headings are mobile! They may be organized the way you feel is best for you! We have already mentioned the cases of *Education* first, second or last, but even *Languages* and *Accomplishments* might be placed differently depending on the effect you want. A typical organization for a recent graduate might be like the one on the left below. But a job with high language content might require reorganization, and even bring language courses in university under the *Languages* heading.

HEADINGS CAN MOVE!

STANDARD STRUCTURE   SPECIAL STRESS

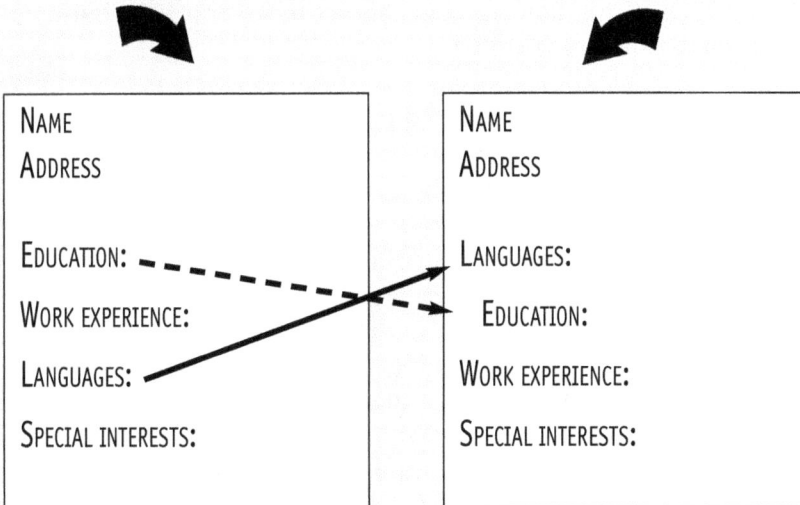

Name
Address

Education:

Work experience:

Languages:

Special interests:

Name
Address

Languages:

Education:

Work experience:

Special interests:

Four Basic Structures for CVs

Now let us look at the four basic structures in detail and understand the advantages and drawbacks of each one.

1. The Chronological CV

The best known structure, the Chronological CV at first seems attractive because it is the easiest to organize. Applicants feel good about it because it represents no challenge – until they start running over onto several pages! They feel that it lays out a kind of history and that history is important. Actually, recruiters are interested in 'history' only if they do not have to interpret it themselves. They want the 'lessons' of history to be clear.

When to USE a chronological CV

Actually, there are many cases in which the Chronological CV is not a good choice. But first, let's take a look at a Chronological CV which works well and study why it is effective in this case. Jacques Driscoll's CV on the following page, shows us several key characteristics of a good chronological CV:

There is a limited number of jobs
Jacques Driscoll has only had three jobs, so he is able to develop each one thoroughly in a little *movie* that focuses on results. Since each job lasted a certain number of years, it suggests good stability and commitment to each job.

All the jobs are in the same field
The CV seems logical to the reader because Driscoll was always in marketing and sales, with added experience in management. Without any other comment by the writer, the recruiter knows that Driscoll is seeking a job in senior management related to sales and marketing, or, at least, in sales management in a different industry.

JACQUES DRISCOLL
96, Ave de Neuilly
75019 Paris
France

WORK EXPERIENCE

1995-Present DIGITAL ELECTONIX
Paris, France.

General Sales Manager: Started as Regional Sales Manager for Southern France. Brought in as General Sales Manager to develop and implement strategies to increase sales to corporate clients in worsening economic climate. Reported directly to CEO. Turned around performance of undermotivated sales management team by redesigning compensation packages and reallocating sales areas in line with sales representatives' profiles. Personally followed major national accounts and strengthened company's position as sole supplier. Sales performance increased by 27%.

1992-1995 PRESSE DIFFUSION
Grenoble, France

District Sales Manager: Worked directly with five magazine wholesalers and dozens of retail accounts to increase circulation of publications. Overcame resistance to innovative publications and gained considerable exposure for breakthrough specialized magazines for the younger set. Added 30% new and profitable accounts to company's line.

1988-1992 DIVERSIFIED PRODUCTS, INC
Hong Kong

Independent Product/Market Representative: Conducted market studies and consulted with sporting goods distributors and retailers of to determine potential demand for Diversified's executive exercise equipment. Concluded existing distribution circuits were ill-adapted to Diversified's specificity and developed contacts with multinational businesses' headquarters to outfit in-house executive health spas. Successfully placed company products with over 100 corporations and ensured after sales service. Left a permanent sales structure.

LANGUAGES

French: mother tongue. English: fluent, four years English selling experience in Honk Kong.

EDUCATION

1987 Master's in Economics and Business,
Catholic University of Lille, France.

The lessons of the 'history' are clear

The reader understands why the writer has organized historically (chronologically) because Driscoll has constantly moved up the ladder, has undergone professional growth. Notice that, although we call it chronological, actually you always put what is most recent first. In reality, it is a reverse chronology. This is important for Driscoll, because he shows his highest position at the top! When reading the CV, the recruiter sees that Driscoll has learned – and profited from that learning. The Chronological CV is perfect for showing promotion into ever greater responsibility. If your last position is not the best, the Chronological CV is not necessarily a good one for you.

In this reverse chronology, the most recent job should be the best

1995-Present	DIGITAL ELECTRONIX Paris, France. **General Sales Manager:**
1992-1995	PRESSE DIFFUSION Grenoble, France **District Sales Manager:**
1988-1992	DIVERSIFIED PRODUCTS, INC Hong Kong **Independent Product/Market Representative:**

The educational background is relatively unimportant to the writer's current career goals

Education is often at the top when the applicant is fresh out of school, or his work experience seems less related to the job he is applying for than his education, possibly in business or management. In Driscoll's CV, as in the CVs of most mature professionals, education is not what shows off his skills the best.

There are no missing years

Obviously, since the chronological CV stresses dates, years of unemployment stand out sharply. 'Interruptions' in a career, whether devoted to personal development or further education fit badly into a chronological structure and raise questions in the mind of a reader who only spends some 20 seconds on scanning it. In Driscoll's case, there are no breaks!

When NOT TO USE a Chronological CV

When the above criteria are not met, it is often wise to structure your CV differently. The chronological form is not useful in the following cases:

When you have had many jobs

A long list of jobs will not be read nor interpreted by recruiters. Detailed descriptions of each will make the CV too long and unattractive. If you have had a lot of jobs in the same field, you should turn to the Knowledge or Experience Areas CV.

When you have worked in very different fields

This situation is typical of most recent graduates who may have worked in a variety of odd jobs to support themselves. These jobs may be coupled with different internships undertaken for vocational training purposes. The whole 'mix' listed chronologically shows no personal or professional development logic and leaves the reader to guess at what the applicant is trying to say about himself. The example of Dieter Schneider's CV on page 177 demonstrates how confusing such a CV might be.

When you are changing professions

Obviously a CV that shows a number of positions in a field that you want to move out of does not help sell skills that you feel you can use in a different field. When you want to convince recruiters that skills you acquired working in a different field are transferable to their business, you would do better to concentrate on the skills themselves, more generically – as in the Knowledge or Experience Areas CV or the Abilities and Achievements CV.

When recent education is important
This may go hand-in-hand with a change in professions. Putting education at the top might be an option, but the jobs following on the CV may not seem linked.

When the lessons of your history are misleading
If your professional career has *not* evolved in a straight line, the chronological CV will only underline the ups and downs. Take the following simplified example, where the applicant has changed jobs too often, has had to take a step down in his last job and also has some years missing.

Was he demoted?

1997-99	Salesman
1993-95	Sales Manager
1991-93	Salesman
1990-91	Salesman
1989-90	Salesman

Where are the missing two years?

Instability?

In this case the chronological CV is *tragic,* doing more harm than good for the applicant. He might have used an entirely different approach that stressed his skills and knowledge of different industries and customers. Even with good job breakdowns added, the hirer will notice immediately:

• that the applicant has moved down from a management position,
• that he had two years of apparent unemployment
• that his time with any one company has often been short.

With any structure of CV, questions about these facts will, of course, be raised in the interview, but the CV – as it is written now – will almost *certainly keep the applicant from reaching the interview stage.* A structure that puts the historical aspects out of the way and allows him to talk about his strong points – *what he knows how to do* – will get him the interview! Then, face-to-face with the recruiter, he can explain in detail the circumstances of his professional history and reinforce the *positive* impression that a better, **interview-winning** CV will have already created.

2. The Skills or Experience Areas CV

This *better,* **interview-winning** CV is often structured along the lines of Skills or Experience Areas. This kind of CV is perfect for overcoming the unfortunate order of events. It allows you to organize experience in 'bundles' or categories of competencies, where the order in which things happened does not matter! Because of that the Skills Areas CV format is very useful in four related cases:

- When you want to *free yourself from a chronology* which is unattractive.

- When you are *starting your career* and want to stress *only* skills and experiences directly related to the job in order to present a *focused* portrait.

- When you are *looking for an internship* and want to prove you have background that would make you operational very quickly.

- When you are *planning a career change* and want to *refocus* your background *away from your past career* and show the skills you have for the new career.

In the case of our salesman above, he would have probably benefited greatly from using a structure like the following:

MANAGEMENT EXPERIENCE

SALES EXPERIENCE

EMPLOYMENT HISTORY
  Company A
  Company B
  Company C

This format frees you from the tyranny of time!

This would permit our salesman to 'free himself' from the slavery of a series of dates that condemn him by their negative suggestions – and still tell the truth! Under the Management heading, he might choose to stress his sales management experience because he is looking for another opportunity at this level. Then, under this heading he can use the job breakdown style to outline the challenges he faced, as well as his contributions. Under the Sales Experience he might wish to point out the various kinds of sales or industries he knows well, with their specific challenges – and the skills he used to overcome them. And the companies he worked for become a simple proof of his experience.

The Skills or Experience Areas CV used for CAREER STARTS

The *Skills or Experience Areas CV* is also often a far more suitable format than the Chronological CV for younger applicants seeking internships or recent graduates looking for an entry-level job. Their experience, whether through internships or just work, has often been acquired in a variety of jobs that do not communicate anything when set out chronologically.

Take the example Dieter Schneider, a German student, ready to graduate, applying for a job in corporate financial analysis with a British bank, who has written the Chronological style CV on the following page. He has done a lot of interesting things, but his CV does not show learning nor make a clear offer of skills! The CV is very confusing, because the recruiter does not know where Dieter is going. He has written his CV this way because he felt "that was how it was supposed to be done!"

There are two major mistakes:

1. His finance experience is not clearly brought to the attention of the recruiter

2. His international experience is scattered throughout the CV instead of being stressed.

Our suggestion to Dieter is to build his CV around two or three main skills areas that make a clear offer to the bank's recruiter, i.e.:

• his knowledge of finance
• his international experience, and
• his understanding of different businesses

FIRST VERSION

Dieter Schneider
Address
Nationality : German, American

> • **Notice how much experience Dieter has abroad.**
> • **His internships have been quite varied but we see no link!**
> • **He is an interesting fellow, but where is he going?**

EDUCATION

1997-Present	FHU Graduate School of Management. Majoring in Finance. Frankfurt, Germany
June 1997	German High School Diploma Arbitur, Otto Bismarck High School, Tübingen, Germany. Participation in student exchange programs in high schools in UK and France.
1994-1996	Exchange program at Harvard Military Academy, Los Angeles, California, USA.

WORK EXPERIENCE

May - Aug 1999	Ceros Ltd., Sheffield, Great Britain Internship in the Marketing Department
Dec - Feb 1999	Nixko Bank, Germany Internship in the M&A department
June - Aug 1998	HSSA Services, Aachen, Germany Internship in the Finance Department
Sept 1997	Martin Euer GmbH & Co, Munich, Germany. Internship in Sales and Logistics.
July & Aug 1996	Motorenwerke; Stuttgart, Germany Internship in the Accounts Department
1997- Present	Part-time work as desk clerk, Marriott Hotel, Tübingen.
1996-97	Part-time work as host and barman for Lufthansa Business Flight Club

FOREIGN STUDIES

Sept - Dec 1999	Notre Dame University, South Dakota, USA. MBA Program
Feb - June 1999	University of Montpellier, France.France

LANGUAGES

German:	Native	English:	Fluent
French:	Good command	Latin:	Good

ACTIVITIES AND MEMBERSHIPS

	Soccer, Badminton, member of School golf team
1998-1999	President of Student's Film club, FHU
1997-present	Member of student association for a political party

Dieter's rewritten CV follows on page 180. In it he has created a *Finance Experience* section where he includes all education and jobs in the field of finance. He has also moved all of his international experience under one heading, included languages (and canceled out Latin). He then adds a small section to show a knowledge of different industries and their workings which will be useful in financial analysis for a bank. To cap it off, he uses **bold type** to draw the reader's attention to the main points painting the portrait of an internationally experienced finance-ready applicant!

The Skills or Experience Areas CV used for Internships

This format of CV is also very useful for applying for internships. Seeking an internship often puts applicants in the uncomfortable situation of having to ask for favors, rather than offering benefits. After all, they are asking for an internship because they need to *learn*, because they are not specialists! A chronological CV often leaves the recruiter uncertain as to why he should hire the writer as a trainee for a couple of months or more. What will the recruiter get in return? The Skills or Experience CV allows the applicant to reorganize everything to point out capabilities and knowledge that will make him useful on the job, and *leave out* extra information that is of no interest to the reader.

What if Dieter Schneider, who wrote the finance-oriented CV on page 177 changes his mind and decides to do an MBA program in the US, instead of going right to work in Finance. He decides he needs more sales experience to ready him for the MBA and applies for a traineeship period in industrial sales in England for the summer. He realizes he is going to have to restructure his CV!

Working on his finance CV, Dieter had learned some very important lessons about organizing information. On page 181, you can see how he rewrote his CV for a Sales job. Before writing, he thought a lot about what a Sales Manager would be looking for when hiring a summer replacement for one of his staff. The manager would want somebody who:

• understood sales logic, even if he was a trainee
• learned to work with new people quickly
• was a good contact person and verbally gifted

- realized the importance in industrial sales of understanding customer problems
- could work with overseas customers

In rebuilding his CV Dieter showed he had contact skills, could talk to customers about their problems, and was aware of marketing issues. *Notice how many things he has given up!* He would have liked to talk about everything he had done, but the reader would not want to read it all. So Dieter put only those experiences he felt were directly linked to sales-related skills.

Like Dieter, when you are looking for your first experience in a field you should always try to show that you are ready for the job, that you have, at least, generic skills and natural aptitudes that will make you quickly operational – in a word, quickly useful! Too often, the word *trainee* is passive; it suggests someone who is taking rather than giving. It is up to you to overcome that negative impression by structuring your CV in a way that convinces the recruiter that you are prepared for the job and will be a fast learner.

The Skills or Experience Areas CV used for CAREER CHANGES

What kind of CV do you write if you have worked five to twenty years in a field and you would like to move into another profession? There is no denying you cannot do it without the skills for the new profession. But as we pointed out in Chapter Three, you often have a variety of generic skills, and often more specific ones, that can be carried over to another profession. The secret is to know how to communicate that clear understanding *you* have of *your* skills to a potential employer!

NEW VERSION
FINANCE

Dieter Schneider
Address

Job Objective: **Financial analyst for Corporate Loans Department of a Bank**

> • **Dieter has specified his objective**
> • **He has built a portrait of a candidate with strong international and finance experience**
> • **He has used bold type for anything that supports that picture**

FINANCE EXPERIENCE

- Currently completing a Master's at FHU Graduate School of Management, Frankfurt, Germany, with a **specialization in Finance**.
- Performed pre-acquisition financial analysis in the **Mergers & Acquisitions** Department, Nixko Bank, Germany. Assigned to Services Acquisitions Team. Wrote up detailed reports on target companies for Services Acquisition Manager. Dec - Feb 1999
- **Assisted Comptroller** of HSSA IT Services, Aachen, Germany in redesigning system to follow outstanding accounts. June - Aug 1998
- **Accounting internship** for Motorenwerke Motors; Stuttgart, Germany. Handled computerized ledger entries. July & Aug 1996

INTERNATIONAL EXPERIENCE

German and American nationality

Working abroad

Ceros, Ltd., Sheffield, **Great Britain**. Marketing Department. Carried out demand and competitor analysis on major EU photocopier markets. Wrote report on recommendations and presented it to Management Committee. May - Aug 1999

Education abroad

- MBA studies at Notre Dame University, South Dakota, **USA**. Sept - Dec 1999
- Economics and Business, University of Montpellier, **France**. Feb - June 1999
- Exchange program at Harvard Military Academy, Los Angeles, California, **USA**. 1994-1996
- Participation in student exchange programs in high schools in **UK** and **France** through my German High School.

Languages

German: native language. English: fluent. French: good command.

KNOWLEDGE OF DIFFERENT BUSINESSES

First-hand experience of Banking, IT Services, Industrial Machinery and Motors, Hotel and Resorts, Photocopiers and Digital Office Automation.

> • **Here Dieter has reorganized everything around Sales!**
>
> • **Original and clear headings!**

Dieter Schneider
Address

Job Objective: **Summer internship in Business to Business Sales**

CONTACT AND COMMUNICATION SKILLS

Good public speaking and easy contact with people from all walks of life and nationalities

- Developed good contact skills **surveying customers** of Cerox Ltd., UK on the phone and in person. Left a positive image of Xerox's service quality with the managers interviewed.

- Made **official presentation** of Ceros survey findings before Management Committee with slides.

- **Worked with students in the USA and France** in MBA studies at Notre Dame University, Indiana, and University of Montpellier, France. **Participated in many exchange programs** in the USA, UK and France since High School

- **Hosted for** Lufthansa Business Flight Club and Marriott Hotel as receptionist/desk clerk with demanding customers.

- **Quickly became accepted team member** of highly specialized teams dealing with sensitive information in accounting and M & A departments.

KNOWLEDGE OF DIFFERENT CUSTOMER PROBLEMS

First-hand experience of Banking, IT Services, Industrial Machinery and Motors, Hotel and Resorts, Herb Processing, Photocopiers and Digital Office Automation.

- Currently completing a Master's at FHU Graduate School of Management, Frankfurt, Germany. Reports made on many industries. **Full program on Sales and Marketing.**

- **Marketing Survey** carried out for Xerox included understanding of customer needs in document storage because of evolution of their markets. May - Aug 1999

- **Sales and Logistics.** Dealt with major international customers in herb and tea sales for Martin Euer GmbH & Co, Munich, Germany. Ensured order follow-up and handled misdelivery problems. Sept 1997

LANGUAGES

Have **worked at high level in English,** German and studied, participated in group work and written reports in French

If we look at the example of Stephanie Furman on page 183, we find a woman who has spent over 20 years in teaching, but who has acquired skills in a variety of areas, such as communication, business and management as well as developed her knowledge of Central Europe. She might well apply for numerous jobs in business communication, tourism and possibly sales in Central Europe. As we can see, a Chronological CV for her would not only be useless, it would be self-defeating!

Her first CV on page 183 makes her experience seem limited to teaching English. The use of *Administration Responsibilities* as a subheading simply reinforces the idea that she knows nothing but the university. The large section devoted to education does not help her, but, once again, gives the profile of an academic! Her real knowledge and skills are *hidden* by her structure.

In the rewritten version on page 184-185, Stephanie has learned to rethink her skills as if she were sitting in front of the recruiter and answering the questions: "What do you know about Central European markets and intercultural problems in management?" So she tells him! She draws on her years of projects in Poland, her research in Central Europe and retailing, her doctoral work, her personal background and languages to rebuild a picture of herself that has a very good chance of taking her to the interview. In preparing her CV as an offer of skills and letting go of her 'history', she has also prepared herself mentally for the interview. She can be positive about what she has to offer.

3. The Abilities and Achievements CV

Another CV structure that is particularly suited to career changes is the *Abilities and Achievements CV.* However, since it is highly targeted to a specific job, it is also useful for applicants who have great experience in one field. A *Chronological CV* for such professionals would simply seem repetitive, and the Skills or Experience Areas CV might only have one heading. With the *Abilities and Achievements* CV, the applicant lays out a direct offer of skills related to the requirements of the job he is applying to and then proves these skills by certain accomplishments. The skills are usually generic, i.e., used or developed in a technical field different from his target position. However, applicants wanting to show quite technical skills acquired in just one field of activity can often use this kind of CV quite effectively. You will find an example of this in Chapter Seven on letter writing.

FIRST VERSION

STEPHANIE FURMAN
Grüneburgweg 6,
D - 6587 Stuttgart
Tel: 49-69-71-33-43-99

WORK EXPERIENCE

1977-Present   **Professor of English**
FHU Graduate School of Management, Stuttgart, Germany

Teaching:

English Business Communication Skills. Design core content, train recruit teachers, constantly update teaching material. Closely follow international events in business, particularly Central Europe

International Business and Negotiation. Created elective course in English on Introduction to International Business. Chose readings, researched subject areas and delivered lectures. Wrote several negotiation cases to sensitize students to issues in international negotiations.

Administration responsibilities:

Coordinated education technology transfers to Polish universities as part of the EU Joint Projects Programs. Organized educational partnerships and raised and administered program funds. Managed faculty teaching assignments for program.

EDUCATION

1999 Doctorate in Intercultural Management, University of Frankfurt, Germany Dissertation on "West European Companies Setting Up on the Polish Market"

1989 Postgraduate degree in Business Administration

1984 Postgraduate degree in English Civilization and Literature

1979 Master's in English

1977 Bachelors in English, Bachelor's in Polish, Bachelor's in Russian

PERSONAL

Married, two children

REWRITTEN VERSION

> **The whole CV stresses Central European development and training skills!**

STEPHANIE FURMAN
Grüneburgweg 6,
D - 6587 Stuttgart
Tel: 49-69-71-33-43-99

Job Objective: Position in Central Europe Market Development and Intercultural Management Training with West European Retailer

E X P E R I E N C E

Central European Markets

Life-long contacts with Poland. For the last ten years, six or more week-long visits to Poland and Hungary. Studied evolution of CE countries to market economies. Wrote several case studies on CE companies privatization and regearing for market competition. Read widely on political developments and rise of modern retailing in Poland, Hungary and the Czech Republic. Doctorate on "West European Companies Setting Up on the Polish Market".

Retailing

Studied the European food retailing market and wrote a business case on the internationalization strategy of Intersection Hypermarkets Group worldwide; special focus on Central Europe. Interviewed and worked closely with top managers in Western Europe and Poland. Special attention given to intercultural management problems and training of CE staff. Case won European Award for Management Education Excellence.

Networking

Developed a span of contacts with officials in Poland and Hungary through technology transfer work. Gained good insight into government business relations in those countries. Constant contacts with European managers through years of research and teaching.

Intercultural Management

Specialized in problems of intercultural management in my research. Close-hand views of problems in transfering work culture and value-systems to CE employees.

Project Management

Years of course planning and teacher management. Handled several technology transfer projects with complete follow-through responsibility from financing, staffing to delivery, reporting and control. Awarded bonus for performance. European authorities refinanced project for three consecutive years.

LANGUAGES:

Polish: Mother tongue, raised by Polish parents, practice in high-level of political and contractual language

Russian: Bachelor's degree. Total comprehension, good conversational ability

English: Totally fluent. Taught English for 20 years. Frequent stays with American friends. Worked on projects with British colleagues.

German: Bilingual German-Polish, secondary, university education and professional life in Germany.

Spanish: Fluent, born and educated in Venezuela until secondary education.

WORK EXPERIENCE

1977-Present   FHU Graduate School of Management, Stuttgart, Germany

Teaching: English Business Communication Skills, International Business and Negotiation.

Management: Coordinated MBA-level technology transfers to Polish universities. Organized educational consortiums and raised funding for programs.

EDUCATION

Doctorate in Intercultural Management, University of Frankfurt, Germany. Postgraduate degrees in Business Administration and English Civilization and Literature. BA and MA in English. Bachelors in both Polish and Russian.

James Mann, who has written the CV on the following page, has chosen the *Abilities and Achievements* structure because a Chronological CV would only point out that he has always been, like Stephanie Furman, a university teacher. He might have used the Skills and Experience Areas CV, but he has learned that for Financial Services Marketing, communication and project management skills are essential. He has a vast experience in communication and projects as well as a good knowledge of finance. Notice how each ability at the top of the CV is supported by an accomplishment presented in job breakdown form in the bottom half of the CV in the Achievements section.

JAMES MANN
2569 Arunda Heights ,Purley
SURREY CR22HF
England

Job Target: **Project Manager for Financial Services Marketing**

ABILITIES
- advising marketing managers on communication approaches to adopt in advertising in English-speaking countries.
- providing professional English-writing services to continental corporations wishing to market their products worldwide.
- full design start to finish of advertising brochures for corporations and universities for overseas.
- writing and recording of professional sales films.
- setting up schedules, performance measurement methods and reporting procedures for team members and debriefing effectively.
- communicating a high level of ideas on financial products and capital markets to demanding publics and leading effective financial negotiations.

ACHIEVEMENTS
- completely conceived and wrote 120 page bulletin for English Graduate School for its overseas marketing purposes.
- wrote scripts and recorded films for major French and Belgian corporations' marketing services.
- translated major French economic treatise on EC for American market.
- planned, organized, and directed management curriculum at major business schools and universities.
- produced schematics, feasibility studies, reports and cost estimates.
- drafted successful bid for EU funding for major educational technology transfer to Eastern Europe.
- managed technology transfer project, including selection of teachers, supervision of course content, payment of all services, and contacts with European partners.
- wrote case studies in organizational design and finance for management education and ran seminars on financial analysis and negotiation.

WORK HISTORY
1985-Present - Associate Professor, International Affairs Dept., Southland University, England
1980-1983 -Instructor of History, UCLA

EDUCATION
1985 - Postgraduate degree in Management, Lille University, France
1983 - Ph.D./ABD, History, UCLA
1974, 78 - B.A., M.A., History, UCLA

The *Abilities and Achievements CV* is probably better suited to applicants with some experience rather than recent graduates, as it requires you to have a large number of skills that can be focused for one particular job. Even if these may be generic, or transferable technical skills, you are more likely to have built them up through years of work experience.

4. The Letter/CV Combination

We have always recommended that applicants send both a CV and a letter. Although many recruiters seem to play down the importance of the letter, they would be shocked not to get one! However, at a *confirmed* level of expertise in a profession, it may seem too 'diluted' to spell out all of your background, education, etc. You may wish to make a highly focused offer of services and get the recruiter involved in your professional background immediately through a direct 'sales talk'. See the example on page 188.

Notice how well this letter/CV suits Gert van Tafeel. He follows up a very direct introduction and offer of services with a short number of highly targeted assignments and their outcomes. The 'tone' of the profile is very assertive and self-confident. Our first impression is that this format of CV could only be used by an experienced manager, offering services at a high level.

However, Internet, as well as the growing international mobility of job applicants in Europe and globally, have made this format of CV an increasingly attractive alternative to the standard *package*. For example, Information Technology Companies are receiving first contacts on the Internet from applicants offering expertise and often advice on solving computer and software problems.[1] The applicants often follow this up with a one-page introduction to themselves, an offer of services and a short work history. This is a *digital* form of the one-page *Letter/CV Combination*. It constitutes a kind of personal profile. With its directness and simplicity, it might be a highly attractive CV to recruiters overloaded with piles of *hardcopy* CV/letter packages.

---

1 See Interview with Carolyn Nimmy, *Cap Gemini*, chapter 2, page 51.

157 Avenue Jan Rays
Rotterdam, Netherlands
October 20, 1999

Mr. Alfred Simpson
CF Consultants
66 Wood Lane, Hempstead
Hertfordshire HP2 4RG
England

Dear Mr. Simpson :

I believe with my wide experience in financial management and counseling, dealing with budgets, planning, forecasting and problem solving I could make a serious contribution to your firm's consulting tasks. Some of my recent achievements are:

Provided financial strategic planning for a large banking institution through careful scanning of the regulatory environment and governmental policy changes. Sold off high-risk assets, reduced off balance sheet items and created innovative financing package to help bank meet new capital adequacy requirements within three years.

Advised corporate clients on prospective acquisitions by thorough analysis of holdings portfolios and past and projected cash flows of target companies. Provided financial engineering services for buyers on both capital and debt markets and assisted clients in non-core business asset sales to quickly reduce debt burden and guarantee acquisitions' viability.

Recruited over 20 finance and economics professionals for banking and corporate clients nearly all of whom moved into senior management positions.

Conducted management seminars on the interpretation of economic and monetary conditions, forecasting models and the use of such data in decision-making.

I hold a Master's in Economics, an International MBA from Tredint University and a Ph.D. degree from IMA.

I would like to meet with you and discuss my future contributions to your firm. I will call you in a week or so.

Sincerely,

G van Tafeel

Gert van Tafeel
32.56.20.10.61

Using the one-page Personal Profile on paper could be risky, if it lands on the desk of a recruiter sifting through a pile of two-page applications. He or she might find you too audacious or feel you are hiding information.

The Letter/CV Combination is often useful when:

- You have <u>confirmed expertise</u> in a field
- When you have <u>very little</u> experience
- When <u>you have been absent</u> from the job market for some time
- When you can <u>find out the name</u> of the person to address it to

Remember, above all, that using the Letter/CV Combination requires *in-depth* research on the company and its developing needs, so you can target your communication to those needs!

Your freedom to choose!

In this Chapter, you have learned that you have a great deal of freedom to choose:

- You know you can put your headings in the order that seems most suitable for your situation and what you want to stress.

- You know you can express your educational level fairly simply despite differences between countries.

- You know that you can talk about work, internships and accomplishments with equal importance as long as they show the skills you are trying to offer.

- You know you can choose from a variety of formats to sell yourself more effectively!

Remember one other lesson: that you can create *headings* that are more suited to your personal case.

Create headings that communicate what you want to say

Don't hesitate to be original when labeling your experience. Originality can be overdone, of course, and in professions where conservatism is valued, your originality should be tempered. Above all, ensure that your headings help the reader understand quickly and clearly!

Many recent graduates, career changers or people coming back on the job market after a long absence often face the difficulty of not finding precise enough headings for their CVs, particularly if they use structures like the *Skills or Experience Areas CV.*

Take the example of one of our Italian post-graduate students who had graduated with a Master's equivalent in Engineering and was doing an M.Sc. equivalent degree in International Business, with a focus on Technology Sales. He had a lot of internships in Engineering, but was very proud of two other accomplishments he did not know how to place:

• one was having organized his class's graduation trip, which he felt was a major management responsibility;
• the other was having worked as a medical receptionist over a year period while he was going to school.

As a matter of fact, he was most proud of the second. He felt he made a major contribution by calmly handling emergency cases effectively; that it was excellent training! We suggested he put his engineering experience at the top for the jobs he was looking for and encouraged him to create the heading "Management-related Experience" to permit him to sell very positively the other two experiences. The 'related' showed that he was sure there was a strong link between what he did and management skills, but he felt 'management' alone might seem arrogant or untrue. He also took his original job title, which was 'President of the Graduation Trip' and used the word *Coordinator* instead. President seemed honorary and elected but did not reflect all the work he had done. Rewritten this way, the CV worked!

ENGINEERING EXPERIENCE

Jan/Feb. 1999   InerG Development, Milan, Italy   **A conventional heading**

Research Laboratory Assistant: Reviewed the findings of a three-year project team and assisted research staff in planning new experiments to ascertain marketable applications.

Aug/Nov. 1998   Axona Detergents Plant, Turin, Italy

Research Engineer: studied and solved a non-quality aspect of detergent production. Conceived, designed and supervised the installation of a mechanical system which was adopted and is still in use. Improved computer operating in control room.

MANAGEMENT-RELATED EXPERIENCE   **An original, yet truthful heading that is very positive**

1998/1999   **Coordinator of Graduating Class Trip to Canada.**

A job title that shows what he really did!

- managed a budget of $100,000 equivalent for over 50 participants
- negotiated with Canadian industries and sponsors
- supervised the publishing of 3000 copies of a 24-page sponsors' brochure.

A job breakdown that makes it clear why this is related to management

1997/1998   **Receptionist** in an emergency medical office.

Managed and organized the schedule of several doctors in an emergency room. Tact and patience were important assets. Handled effectively a large number of high-pressure emergency cases.

Now you have a good idea of the latitude you have in structuring your CV to set off the skills you inventoried in Chapter Three, and show the accomplishments you learned how to communicate in Chapter Four. You should now try out a variety of structures and make careful choices about what to include and what <u>not</u> to include. It will take you many hours to get a CV that does what you want it to do. Above all, show it to several friends and tell them what you are hoping to communicate. Ask for critical advise, rather than congratulations. It will only be looked at once by a recruiter. Does it work?

When you have decided on the structures best suited to the jobs you are seeking and written the *movies* you want the recruiter to see, turn to Chapter Six to learn how to write a cover letter that links your skills with the accomplishments on your CV and makes an offer of benefits!

INTERVIEW #7 :
AT PHILIPS WE WANT TO SEE IF A CANDIDATE'S SKILLS ARE TRANSFERABLE TO US

Interview with Jo Pieters, International Human Resource Management Consultant, Philips, Netherlands. Responsible for Coordination of Global MBA Recruitment.

▶ **What do you look for in an applicant's CV ?**

Transferability is the key word. We look to see if what applicants have done in the past is *transferable* to us. Philips is an industrial company and experience in an industrial company is essential to us. We want to see how applicants' experience translates for our company, for our business. If their working experience is not directly related to our business, we look at the projects they have handled to see if their skills are transferable. We are not interested so much in the projects themselves, but in their contributions to those projects. What was their role in getting the project accomplished?
We also stress Six Leadership Competencies. They are:

- Shows determination to achieve excellent results
- Focuses on the market
- Finds better ways
- Demands top performance
- Inspires commitment
- Develops self and others

This keeps us from digging through what every person has done and what they want to say about themselves. If a person has done something, we want him or her to prove it. Then we look at how what they have done corresponds to the leadership competencies we seek. Then we will interview them to get evidence of these competencies.

▶ **How should applicants go about writing their CVs?**

We prefer a one-page CV. This is also usually what is published by the Management schools graduation class books. We look through the books published by Wharton, IMD, INSEAD, etc. Since we look through some 3000 to 4000 CVs, applicants have to be immediately clear on what they are offering. When they come to our campus, applicants may often bring a somewhat more elongated version of what they have done.

Applicants should know how to focus on the major issues and leave out unuseful information, leave out anything that is not relevant to the recruiter. They should be precise and compact, and always say what roles they played, more than talk about the projects themselves.

99% of MBA graduates want to move into general management, and we understand that fully. However, companies like ours will not give them a general management position right from the beginning. This might be the case with consulting companies or investment banking. At Philips, those positions will come later. We often regret that the person writing did not take one step back and ask himself "What is the added value I am offering the company today?" Prove by your performance what you are capable of doing today, what added value you are bringing in today. We are not recruiting for a career, but for what you can do for us now, where you will start today!

This means that applicants should improve their homework on the company. They should be able to put themselves in our shoes and think about what kind of person we are looking for, as we are neither investment bankers nor consultants. Their offer should become very clear in the two minutes we may spend on the CV.

▶ How important is the cover letter for you?

In my case, as I concentrate on recruiting MBA graduates, in 99% there is no letter, because the CV comes from the MBA school book. The offer they are making will have to be clear in the CV. We also go to the campuses and the students can find out directly from us what we are seeking.

▶ Is the Internet CV becoming more frequent?

Not much more than before. They seem to have stabilized. Persons applying to Philips seem to know how and who we recruit, that we draw on the school books. When we do get a digital CV, we expect the same format as on hard copy. The CV is always the same entrance ticket which allows one chance only. We do not scan or even keep CVs, unless the person has been interviewed.

▶ How frequently do applicants lie?

Most of our applicants are bright, very smart. They have done their homework and know what we want, so they have no need to lie. They also know that professionals would see right through them if they lied. We would dig a bit during the interview and we would be able to tell that something was a lie. Then it would all be over, just like that!

Applicants sometimes 'package' reality so as to embellish it, to make it more positive. We expect that and find it normal; after all, it is good salesmanship, and they will be selling our products and their ideas. In any case, if you do not know how to sell, it will show in the first 3 minutes of the interview.

Key points in chapter five

- The most important information to put on a CV is your education, your languages, your experience and your accomplishments.

- In Europe most recruiters understand the differences in the education systems.

- You can talk about both your internships and your jobs on a CV to show your skills and what you have learned.

- Show that you can use your languages in an active way.

- There are many different structures possible for a CV.

- Les informations indispensables dans un CV sont : votre formation, vos langues, vos expériences, vos réalisations.

- Bon nombre de recruteurs européens connaissent les différences entre les systèmes éducatifs en Europe.

- Vous pouvez utilisez indifféremment vos emplois et stages passés pour faire valoir vos compétences et les apprentissages réalisés.

- Montrez votre capacité à utiliser les langues de manière plus active que vous ne le faites quand vous écrivez : lu, écrit, parlé !

- Il y a différentes structures de CV possibles.

- Choose the kind of CV that shows your skills the best.

- The Chronological CV is best when you have progressed steadily.

- The Skills or Experience Areas CV is best when you need to show two or three major knowledge areas.

- The Abilities and Achievements CV is best when you want to focus on abilities used in a variety of circumstances that are suited to one particular job.

- The Letter/CV combination is useful when you want to make a very personal offer of services to a company you know well.

- Create personal headings instead of using standard ones.

- Choisissez le style et format de CV qui vous permettent de mieux montrer vos compétences.

- Le format chronologique est le plus approprié lorsque votre progression professionnelle a été constante et régulière.

- Le CV zone de compétences ou d'expérience est plus adapté quand vous avez deux ou trois domaines de connaissances à faire valoir.

- L'approche du CV organisé selon vos capacités/ réalisations est plus appropriée lorsque vous avez acquis des savoir-faire utilisables dans un emploi spécifique en diverses circonstances.

- Le document unique CV/Lettre est surtout à utiliser lorsque votre offre est très personnelle ou si elle est faite à une entreprise que vous connaissez très bien par ailleurs.

- N'hésitez pas à créer vos propres rubriques et à ne pas utiliser systématiquement les titres standards.

CV Layout and Typing

All of the four CV types we have studied deserve the best possible layout for good effect. But what is good effect? The answer is that the CV should be easy to read! The different structures themselves exist to make it easy for the recruiter to find what you want him to find in the right order. The structure is the most important part of layout. All the rest becomes a question of typing and choice of fonts or characters.

THE PURPOSE OF WHITE

Over the years, we have asked our seminar participants: "What is the purpose of white?" They don't always understand the question, so we hold up two CVs: one with very little information on it, and the other covered with black print. Then they usually understand that a good CV should not be all white; it should have enough black print on it to be interesting, have something to say. On the other hand, a CV loaded with black is unreadable, because it is aggressive and frightens the reader away. You will notice that all four of the CV types on the next page have **enough white to make the black easy to access**.

Too much white, on the other hand, comes often from just making a 'list' CV, with no job breakdowns. Such CVs quickly find their way into the trash.

Too much black comes from not knowing how to sacrifice some information, how to prioritize – and from over-formatting the document with word-processing effects.

Chronological

JACQUES DRISCOLL
96, Ave de Neuilly
75019 Paris
France

WORK EXPERIENCE
1995-Present   DIGITAL ELECTONIX
                Paris, France.

> **General Sales Manager:** Started as Regional Sales Manager for Southern France. Brought in as General Sales Manager to develop and implement strategies to increase sales to corporate clients in worsening economic climate. Reported directly to CEO. Turned around performance of undermotivated sales management team by redesigning compensation packages and reallocating sales areas in line with sales representatives' profiles. Personally followed major national accounts and strengthened company's position as sole supplier. Sales performance increased by 27%.

1992-1995   PRESSE DIFFUSION
                Grenoble, France

> **District Sales Manager:** Worked directly with five magazine wholesalers and dozens of retail accounts to increase circulation of publications. Overcame resistance to innovative publications and gained considerable exposure for breakthrough specialized magazines for the younger set. Added 30% new and profitable accounts to company's line.

1988-1992   DIVERSIFIED PRODUCTS, INC
                Hong Kong

> **Independent Product/Market Representative:** Conducted market studies and consulted with sporting goods distributors and retailers of to determine potential demand for Diversified's executive exercise equipment. Concluded existing distribution circuits were ill-adapted to Diversified's specificity and developed contacts with multinational businesses' headquarters to outfit in-house executive health spas. Successfully placed company products with over 100 corporations and ensured after sales service. Left a permanent sales structure.

LANGUAGES
        French: mother tongue. English: fluent, four years English selling experience in Honk Kong.

EDUCATION
1987   Master's in Economics and Business,
            Catholic University of Lille, France.

Skills or Experience Areas

Dieter Schneider
Address

Job Objective: **Financial analyst for**
Corporate Loans Department of a Bank

FINANCE EXPERIENCE
- Currently completing a Master's at FHU Graduate School of Management, Frankfurt, Germany, with a **specialization in Finance**.
- Performed pre-acquisition financial analysis in the **Mergers & Acquisitions** Department, Nixko Bank, Germany. Assigned to Services Acquisitions Team. Wrote up detailed reports on target companies for Services Acquisition Manager. Dec - Feb 1999
- **Assisted Comptroller** of HSSA IT Services, Aachen, Germany in redesigning system to follow outstanding accounts. June - Aug 1998
- **Accounting Internship** for Motorenwerke Motors; Stuttgart, Germany. Handled computerized ledger entries. July & Aug 1996

INTERNATIONAL EXPERIENCE
        German and American nationality

Working abroad
        Ceros, Ltd., Sheffield, **Great Britain**. Marketing Department. Carried out demand and competitor analysis on major EU photocopier markets. Wrote report on recommendations and presented it to Management Committee. May - Aug 1999

Education abroad
- MBA studies at Notre Dame University, South Dakota, **USA**. Sept - Dec 1999
- Economics and Business, University of Montpellier, **France**. Feb - June 1999
- Exchange program at Harvard Military Academy, Los Angeles, California, USA. 1994-1996
- Participation in student exchange programs in high schools in **UK** and **France** through my German High School.

Languages
        German: native language. English: fluent. French: good command.

KNOWLEDGE OF DIFFERENT BUSINESSES
First-hand experience of Banking, IT Services, Industrial Machinery and Motors, Hotel and Resorts, Photocopiers and Digital Office Automation.

Abilities & Achievements

JAMES MANN
2569 Arunda Heights ,Purley   Job Target: **Project**
SURREY CR22HF   **Manager for Financial**
England   **Services Marketing**

ABILITIES
- advising marketing managers on communication approaches to adopt in advertising in English-speaking countries.
- providing professional English-writing services to continental corporations wishing to market their products worldwide.
- full design start to finish of advertising brochures for corporations and universities for overseas.
- writing and recording of professional sales films.
- setting up schedules, performance measurement methods and reporting procedures for team members and debriefing effectively.
- communicating a high level of ideas on financial products and capital markets to demanding publics and leading effective financial negotiations.

ACHIEVEMENTS
- completely conceived and wrote 120 page bulletin for English Graduate School for its overseas marketing purposes.
- wrote scripts and recorded films for major French and Belgian corporations' marketing services.
- translated major French economic treatise on EC for American market.
- planned, organized, and directed management curriculum at major business schools and universities.
- produced schematics, feasibility studies, reports and cost estimates.
- drafted successful bid for EU funding for major educational technology transfer to Eastern Europe.
- managed technology transfer project, including selection of teachers, supervision of course content, payment of all services, and contacts with European partners.
- wrote case studies in organizational design and finance for management education and ran seminars on financial analysis and negotiation.

WORK HISTORY
1985-Present - Associate Professor, International Affairs Dept., Southland University, England
1980-1983 -Instructor of History, UCLA

EDUCATION
1985 - Postgraduate degree in Management, Lille University, France
1983 - Ph.D./ABD, History, UCLA
1974, 78 - B.A., M.A., History, UCLA

Letter/CV Combination

                                        157 Avenue Jan Rays
                                        Rotterdam, Netherlands
                                        October 20, 1999

Mr. Alfred Simpson
CF Consultants
66 Wood Lane, Hempstead
Hertfordshire HP2 4RG
England

Dear Mr. Simpson :

I believe with my wide experience in financial management and counseling, dealing with budgets, planning, forecasting and problem solving I could make a serious contribution to your firm's consulting tasks. Some of my recent achievements are:

> Provided financial strategic planning for a large banking institution through careful scanning of the regulatory environment and governmental policy changes. Sold off high-risk assets, reduced off balance sheet items and created innovative financing package to help bank meet new capital adequacy requirements within three years.

> Advised corporate clients on prospective acquisitions by thorough analysis of holdings portfolios and past and projected cash flows of target companies. Provided financial engineering services for buyers on both capital and debt markets and assisted clients in non-core business asset sales to quickly reduce debt burden and guarantee acquisitions' viability.

> Recruited over 20 finance and economics professionals for banking and corporate clients nearly all of whom moved into senior management positions.

> Conducted management seminars on the interpretation of economic and monetary conditions, forecasting models and the use of such data in decision-making.

I hold a Master's in Economics, an International MBA from Tredint University and a Ph.D. degree from IMA.

I would like to meet with you and discuss my future contributions to your firm. I will call you in a week or so.

                                        Sincerely,

                                        G van Tafeel

                                        Gert van Tafeel
                                        32.56.20.10.61

200

TYPING

Punctuation

This is not a book on how to type, so we will only be interested in some punctuation aspects. A CV is not like this book, which uses quotation marks, inverted commas, colons, semi-colons, exclamation marks, etc. If you read over the many CVs included in this book, you will find that most complex punctuation is avoided. Most of the time, the writers have used only commas and periods in their sentences and, occasionally, colons after their headings. There is no reason to quote anything or anybody on a CV or in a letter. Sentences, to be scannable, should use only commas for their pauses, not semi-colons. These would only slow the reader down. Commas can also be used to separate adjectives or lists of things. Most sentences should be simple sentences. If there are two ideas, they should be broken into two sentences for fast reading.

Parentheses?

Parentheses are something to be avoided in CVs, and even more in letters. They confuse the eye and stop the reading. They are often used abusively, when people do not know how to structure the sentence in another way. Remember that parentheses are reserved for illustrative, relatively unimportant information, or for secrets! You will see that there are no parentheses on any of the CVs or letters in this book, because everything the people wrote was important.

FORMATING AND EFFECTS

Some of the greatest crimes in CV-writing are committed when the applicants choose from all the capabilities of modern word-processors or desktop publishing software. They just cannot give up some of the great effects made possible by the computer, and they tend to turn out CVs that look like modern art. You have an example of highly overdone formatting applied to Jacques Driscoll's Chronological CV on the following page. This is nothing compared to the effects that some candidates use! Driscoll himself, of course, is much too focused on 'talking business' to resort to such modern art. His own CV was sober and easy to read. Word-processors also come with pre-formatted layouts that are often excessive.

This is unreadable!

JACQUES DRISCOLL
96, Ave de Neuilly
75019 Paris
France

WORK EXPERIENCE

1995-Present	DIGITAL ELECTONIX Paris, France.

General Sales Manager: Started as Regional Sales Manager for Southern France. Brought in as General Sales Manager to develop and implement strategies to increase sales to corporate clients in worsening economic climate. Reported directly to CEO. Turned around performance of undermotivated sales management team by redesigning compensation packages and reallocating sales areas in line with sales representatives' profiles. Personally followed major national accounts and strengthened company's position as sole supplier. Sales performance increased by 27%.

1992-1995	PRESSE DIFFUSION Grenoble, France

District Sales Manager: Worked directly with five magazine wholesalers and dozens of retail accounts to increase circulation of publications. Overcame resistance to innovative publications and gained considerable exposure for breakthrough specialized magazines for the younger set. Added 30% new and profitable accounts to company's line.

1988-1992	DIVERSIFIED PRODUCTS, INC Hong Kong

Independent Product/Market Representative: Conducted market studies and consulted with sporting goods distributors and retailers of to determine potential demand for Diversified's executive exercise equipment. Concluded existing distribution circuits were ill-adapted to Diversified's specificity and developed contacts with multinational businesses' headquarters to outfit in-house executive health spas. Successfully placed company products with over 100 corporations and ensured after sales service. Left a permanent sales structure.

LANGUAGES:

French: mother tongue. English: fluent, four years English selling experience in Hong Kong.

EDUCATION:

1987	Master's in Economics and Business, Catholic University of Lille, France.

Remember to draw attention to yourself by ideas and precision, not formatting. Most CVs should be very sober. Lines, boxes and shadows just slow the reader down.

Choice of Fonts

The reader can also be slowed down by a bad choice of fonts. In the example on the previous page the formatter has gone wild! Movie-picture billboard type fonts have been mixed with scripts that attempt to imitate handwriting. You will notice that all the CVs in this book are either in Times or Arial fonts. Times, or similar serif fonts, are known for their readability and are used in books for that reason. Arial or Helvetica type fonts are often used for titles, but may also be used to good effect in short documents. Some companies like them for their letters. Fonts that draw too much attention should be avoided. You do not want the reader to see your fonts; you want him to see your ideas!

Bullets

Word-processing has also brought us an incredible variety of bullets to embellish our presentations. Although a lot of them may be very helpful in setting off ideas in slide presentations, sales talks, multimedia advertising and Internet pages, most of them are too powerful for CVs. Simple bullets like the following might be suitable-if no bigger than 12 points:

● ❑ ■

Bullets like the following distract the reader from what you are saying!

❤ ➡ ✔ ❖ ● ⇨ ⇛

Bold and Italics

Italics do not contribute much to a CV and, indeed, may slow the reader down. Bold type may be very useful if you do no use it too much. Its purpose is to stress certain things, to say they are the most important things in a paragraph or on a line. Remember that the companies you have worked for are not the most important things on a CV! Many people use both capitals and bold type for the name of the company and then their job title is almost hidden. Bold should be used for what *you did*, particularly things related to the job you are seeking. On the other hand, if you find you are bolding everything, then do not use it at all!

If you look back to Chapter Five, you will notice that bold type can be used very effectively. First of all, it can make the headings of your CV stand out, so the recruiter can find what he wants quickly. Jacques Driscoll used bold very little but very effectively: he only **bolded** his job titles.

Remember Dieter Schneider? Dieter used a very different approach, because he was not using job titles. He **bolded** his job objectives and he also **bolded** all the words in his two different CVs that stressed either international skills, or finance and sales skills respectively. Those **bolded** areas guided the reader quickly through demonstrations that Dieter was ready for the job he was asking for.

In the section on the text page, taken from his Sales CV, Dieter has **bolded** short phrases to build up a picture of someone who has good contact and communications skills, and therefore ready to move into selling.

CONTACT AND COMMUNICATION SKILLS

Good public speaking and easy contact with people from all walks of life and nationalities

- Developed good contact skills **surveying customers** of Xerox Ltd., UK on the phone and in person. Left a positive image of Xerox's service quality with the managers interviewed.

- Made **official presentation** of Xerox survey findings before Management Committee with slides.

- **Worked with students in the USA and France** in MBA studies at Notre Dame University, Indiana, and University of Montpellier, France. **Participated in many exchange programs** in the USA, UK and France since High School

- **Hosted for** Lufthansa Business Flight Club and Marriott Hotel as receptionist/desk clerk with demanding customers.

- **Quickly became accepted team member** of highly specialized teams dealing with sensitive information in accounting and M & A departments.

INTERNET AND SCANNABLE CVS

Internet and all other electronic technology have changed CV-writing very little. There are books being published that teach you how to write CVs for the Internet, or CVs that can be machine-scanned and then processed by artificial intelligence to draw up a list of candidates with the right profile. We do not criticize these books, but in our interviews with companies we have learned that *there are only two ways in which such technology might affect how you write your CV:*

1. the formatting you use, and
2. the words you use

Remember that the self-discovery process we have gone through does not change! The job breakdown does not change. The structure you give your CV does not change. The approach you take in your letter does not change. The formatting we have suggested does not change.

Formatting

Formatting for the Internet should keep the same simplicity and readability for obvious reasons, even if you want to show off your capability to build an interactive home page with hypertext for more detailed experience descriptions or a possible video. All of these effects depend on your own Internet-smartness!

Formatting for scanning technology requires the same simplicity we have mentioned above. Although scanners do read bold type, they do not read special fonts well, nor shadow effects or lines. 'Wallpapers' you download from the Internet do not make as good a background for a CV as simple white paper. These wallpapers do not scan well and also keep the scanner from 'seeing' the text.

The CV on page 208 is unscannable because of its wallpaper background but also because of the script font used. Even without digital technology, it is unreadable!

Writing to a scanner...

Action verbs and adjectives remain the same on a scannable CV as they do on a hard copy one. The only thing that might change is that key words for the company, or key words for the position you are seeking, should be repeated. Whereas Dieter Schneider **bolded** aspects of his experience related to finance or sales in his two CVs, for scanning technology he would be tempted to calculate *which words* should appear 3 or 4 times in his CV. For his sales CV, those might be 'sales', 'customers', 'negotiation', etc. The problem in writing such a CV is that it might become impoverished from a deeper communication standpoint. It might lose out in finesse.

Smart candidates learn to adapt to such technology. They may go on Internet to the home pages of companies they are targeting and learn the *buzzwords* that the company uses over and over again. These buzzwords often reoccur either in its recruitment pages or in its annual reports. All of these documents can often be downloaded! Then the candidates build these words into their CVs so that the scanner selects them as candidates with the right profile.

If this is what it takes, do it! But do not sacrifice all of the steps of skills inventorying and job breakdowns we have worked on, because you will need all you have prepared at the interview. You will also need it to write your hard copy CV. At one stage or another in any recruiting process you will be asked for your hardcopy CV!

Be careful not to count only on the repetition of certain words. You might paint a picture of yourself which is not true, and which you cannot defend.[1]

---

1 See interview with Veli-Pekka Niitamo, *Nokia Telecommunications*, Chapter 6, page 209.

Unscannable!

JAMES MANN
2569 Arunda Heights ,Purley
SURREY CR22HF
England

Job Target: **Project Manager for Financial Services Marketing**

ABILITIES:
- advising marketing managers on communication approaches to adopt in advertising in English-speaking countries.
- providing professional English-writing services to continental corporations wishing to market their products worldwide.
- full design start to finish of advertising brochures for corporations and universities for overseas.
- writing and recording of professional sales films.
- setting up schedules, performance measurement methods and reporting procedures for team members and debriefing effectively.
- communicating a high level of ideas on financial products and capital markets to demanding publics and leading effective financial negotiations.

ACHIEVEMENTS:
- completely conceived and wrote 120 page bulletin for English Graduate School for its overseas marketing purposes
- wrote scripts and recorded films for major French and Belgian corporations' marketing services
- translated major French economic treatise on E.C. for American market
- planned, organized, and directed management curriculum at major business schools and universities
- produced schematics, feasibility studies, reports and cost estimates.
- drafted successful bid for EU funding for major educational technology transfer to Eastern Europe.
- managed technology transfer project, including selection of teachers, supervision of course content, payment of all services, and contacts with European partners.
- wrote case studies in organizational design and finance for management education and ran seminars on financial analysis and negotiation.

WORK HISTORY :
1985-Present - Associate Professor, International Affairs Dept., Southland University, England
1980-1983 -Instructor of History, UCLA

EDUCATION :
1985 - Postgraduate degree in Management, Lille University, France
1983 - Ph.D./ABD, History, UCLA
1974, 78 - B.A., M.A., History, UCLA

INTERVIEW # 8:
INTERNET HAS CHANGED THE WAY NOKIA RECRUITS

Interview with Veli-Pekka Niitamo, Head of Global Resourcing, Nokia Telecommunications, Finland

▶ **What is Nokia's approach to processing CVs from applicants ?**

At Nokia, the CV is not an issue. We have a different view on applications and hiring than most companies and identify competencies in a different way. Writing a CV has too often become an art and has nothing to do with the candidate's skills. Candidates may be very 'slick' when writing their CVs, and then we find the interview does not match the portrait the candidates presented. That is why most graduates enter our company *electronically*. We have developed an Internet job application system which is operational both nationally in Finland and in Northern Europe, a system we are gradually developing for the rest of the world.

Candidates to Nokia fill out questionnaires on line, questionnaires that probe for very specific job area competencies. This system is a way of sorting out people with real competencies from those who are just bragging. We also attract top candidates through Internet competitions, donations, R&D projects, and internship programmes. Therefore, we are able to reliably evaluate their competencies over a period of time. We seek out applicants from the top technological universities in Northern Europe and elsewhere.

CVs are requested from applicants at a later stage of the recruitment process – before the interview. It serves as a quick sort out when there are too many good applications or too many bad ones. The CV will help us determine whether the person was bragging or not in filling out the Internet application. After that, we put the applicants through assessment tests. Then, the manager the person will be working with will study the CV, the self evaluation, the key competencies and the assessment made by the previous interviewers. Only then, will the applicant be interviewed by his future manager.

▶ **Do you find there are cultural differences in the way applicants write CVs?**

Indeed! In the US, for instance, we are confronted with a more 'subjective' approach in a country where the CV or resume format is the rule. In Germany, on the other hand, we find less subjectivity. At Nokia, we try to adapt our assessment country by country and read behind the words, evaluating the way people present their skills in their country!

- **In Northern Europe**, Internet first-stage recruiting is quite developed, thus Nokia only recruits over the net. Our applicants are technology smart and therefore able to self-evaluate themselves against the competency requirements of a vacancy on-line. This has tremendously reduced recruitment time. In some cases, the hiring manager has called a candidate in 5 minutes after his web application was filed.

- **In the USA**, CVs have remained the rule and people are used to writing them. Applicants use certain tools to write CVs. We fear that because of those tools, the CVs do not reflect the candidate's real competencies: they are just smart writers! But for global candidates we still use the CV or resume format, hoping to make it evolve globally.

Our knowledge of cultural habits is pretty good. We will be able to tell whether the person was overselling or not and, knowing his country of origin, we can correct for the national reasons for which he or she exaggerated.

▶ How do you differentiate between lying and 'overselling'?

We are fully aware that because of their education and upbringing some nationalities under-stress and others overstress. For example, underselling is typical for the Finns, Scandinavians, or the mainland Chinese. On the other hand, Americans oversell, as do American-educated Chinese.

▶ How do you feel about the scannable CV?

Scanning a CV is just another technology. However, in cases of persons trained in writing scannable CVs for artificial intelligence scan reading, it can lead to abuses. In this case, 'overselling' can be quite dangerous. Sometimes, when we get down studying applicants' specific competencies, we realize that some have written, for example, the word 'Java programming' seven times in their CVs, which will cause our software to rank them as attractive candidates. We are suspicious of this and may feel that it is artificial or that they are exaggerating. Maybe they are applying directly what they read out of a book. In these cases, we ask them specific questions either face-to-face, or on-line, and, when we realize that they cannot answer these questions ad-hoc they are automatically discarded.

▶ Is the letter important for you?

We ask graduates for letters when they are in their final stage of selection. Then both the letter and how they write it become criteria. The letter shows their motivation, their interest, We may probe things like their rationale for wanting to work in Finland when their country of origin is California. This kind of information becomes relevant.

We do get a lot of e-mail applicants. Unfortunately, they usually mass mail and do not tailor, or poorly tailor, the letters they send us. Certainly very few know how to connect their letter to their CV. This gives the impression they lack motivation.

In the end, a good CV and a good cover letter are very important. Don't try to outsmart artificial intelligence – no Java programs – be sincere! Tell the truth, be careful of 'buzzwords' because we can see right through them.

Key points in chapter six

- Leave enough white background on your CV so the recruiter can read the black text easily.

- Use very little punctuation on a CV.

- Format your CV layout and type for easy reading.

- Only use **bold** type to show off yourself and your skills.

- Internet and scanning technology have not changed the way you should write a CV.

- Make sure your CV is easy to scan.

- Laissez suffisamment de blanc dans votre CV pour que le "noir" ressorte

- Utilisez très peu de ponctuations dans un CV.

- La mise en forme choisie doit permettre une lecture facile.

- Utilisez les caractères **gras** uniquement pour vous décrire ou faire état de vos compétences.

- L'Internet et la technologie du CV scanné ne doivent pas changer l'approche que vous devez avoir vis-à-vis de votre CV.

- Assurez-vous que votre CV est facile à scanner.

How to write the letter

Our purpose in this Chapter is not to repeat what we said in Chapter Three concerning the relationship between the letter and the CV. Here we are going to deal with the actual *structuring* of the letter and *drafting* of the paragraphs. Yet, one key point needs to be reiterated: the letter needs to *make an offer of benefits*!

The letter can be a crucial plus, but not for applicants who write letters that are commonplace, empty and boring. The problem is that you often feel you have said everything in the CV, especially if you have mastered the art of writing a CV, chosen the right structure for your situation and written job breakdowns that provide clear 'movies' of your accomplishments. So the letter seems *useless*. You may truly be tempted to write simply: "Read my CV".

In truth, the letter is your *second chance* to strengthen the picture the recruiter has of your skills! If you have structured your CV correctly, you have already shown that you understand the employer's business, because you have set off the skills that go with his needs. But the letter can draw attention to these skills very directly; it can, *like a good salesman*, underline three or four major advantages of hiring you that will be supported, demonstrated, spelled out, by the CV!

THE LETTER IS A SALES TALK !

Imagine you are selling a car, or a machine, or even a house! You are giving a *guided tour* to the customer. As you walk through the house you can point out the advantages of the house very concretely, because the buyer has them in front of him. Your letter is your sales talk and your CV is the house. Would you just let the buyers walk through without you? Would you give up the advantage of pointing out that the size of the kitchen is perfect for their life style, that the number of bedrooms is a real plus for a growing family? The advantage of having the recruiter in front of your CV is that you can guide him through it. If you simply write "Read my CV", it sends the reader to the CV *in place of the letter; the conversation stops*! In a <u>good</u> letter, *each sentence* should draw attention to the strong points of your application, *develop* what is said on the CV!

You will think: "But, aren't I just repeating my CV, saying the same things again? Isn't that boring, stupid?"

The answer is, of course, that you are not saying the same things again. You are using the language of skills, self-knowledge, learning and growth! You are going to be drawing on your skills and personality inventory and linking the performance shown on your CV with the person talking in the letter. Let's move on to the different paragraphs of the letter to see how you should work. We will refer to the letter written by Marie Taillat on the following page.

CONTENT OF THE LETTER

The opening paragraph

Remember that in business correspondence, all important information should be *up front*! Busy people do not like letters that read like mysteries; they want to know what you want from the very beginning! A good first paragraph should tell the reader why you are writing, should identify you and why you are writing to his or her organization. The following opening by Marie Taillat, a student seeking a summer job, is simple and 'straight-to-the-point'.

> I have been told that Canon, Inc. is looking for students to conduct surveys about your new photocopier range. I think I am in a good position to apply for this job.

Marie Taillat
123, rue Victor Hugo
14800 Trouville, France
tel: 33-2-15-49-74-89
mtaillat@email.com

April 15, 1999

Pieter Tiemens
Marketing Manager
Canon,
Netherlands

Dear Mr. Tiemens,

I have been told that Canon, Inc. is looking for students to conduct surveys about your new photocopier range. I think I am in a good position to apply for this job.

A series of courses devoted to marketing research in my Business School have provided me with a solid theoretical foundation for such work. Many class exercises in working up questionnaires, processing statistical data and reporting succinctly on findings have prepared me for both desk research and field work. I also recently took part in a nation-wide survey of French business leaders, which made me operational in conducting business surveys from the exploratory phase to the final report.

I feel I have developed good contact skills, whether dealing with customers or suppliers. Working in sales brought me in touch with many managers and taught me to listen well to customer problems and get valuable information to report to the home office. Whether as a member of a team, or in the field, I have learned to assertively offer creative and useful suggestions, while maintaining good relations with my co-workers.

I have been reading up on developments in the European photocopier market to prepare myself for the opportunity to work for you. I know the competition is tough and that digital technology is reconfiguring the industry. I would like to have the chance to learn more about this industry by carrying through a research project for you.

I hope to be hearing from you soon.

Yours sincerely,

Marie Taillat

Marie Taillat

Encl: Personal CV

Each sentence reinforces a part of the CV!

The reader learns four things right away:

1. The writer is a student
2. She wants a temporary job
3. She is offering to carry out market surveys
4. She feels qualified

The tone is very positive and targeted, *no time is wasted*; so the reader is curious to go on to the next paragraph, even if he isn't looking for students to carry out surveys, because he knows he will not get lost in a meandering, confusing letter with a lot of *pointless* information. We will take a look at the rest of the letter later.

Another example is of a student looking for an internship to advance his career plans for finance.

> I have become acquainted with your bank through a survey I performed last summer. Mr. Braun from X Bank advised me to apply to your bank because we both believe that I can be a useful assistant in your commercial financial products department this coming summer. I hope to go into banking finance and an opportunity with your bank would give me insight into your specifically international view of products whose importance is increasing in European business. Please let me tell you why I can be of use to your bank.
>
> First,...

He has written a longer introduction, but which flows easily and quickly to his selling points. He stresses his knowledge of the bank and introduces a contact person who is known to the reader. If Mr. Braun were not known to the receiver of the letter, our student could write, for example:

> Mr. Braun, Financial Products Manager of the Dresdner Bank in ....., who supervised my internship, advised me...

In this case, Mr. Braun becomes a referee or reference the recruiter can contact for information about the applicant, if he wishes. Then, in the opening paragraph, our future intern moves onto two important ideas with lightening speed:

- He will be useful
- He has career plans in finance
- What he wants in return: learning!

Both of these opening paragraphs have been written by applicants for temporary jobs or traineeships rather than for full-time career starts or career moves. Yet the approach can be the same in the latter cases. Above all, they say who they are, what they want and what they are offering, then send the reader quickly on to the 'meat of the matter'. They avoid long, complicated explanations that put a reader to sleep; there is no undue flattery; and service is offered in a confident tone. The rest of their letters is going to tell the recruiter why they can bring benefits to the company.

Let's take a look Marie Taillat's whole letter again, on page 221, and pick up some important pointers about how she develops her skills.

The skills paragraphs

She has built her letter carefully, like a sales argument. Paragraphs 2 and 3 talk about her skills in some detail. In paragraph 4 she comes back to the recruiting company and its business, reinforcing her appeal by showing that she is really motivated through the efforts she has made. She has not worked in the photocopier market before, but she has replaced this experience to a degree by curiosity and preparation. She finishes by repeating her request for a job and directly linking it with a service she is offering! She concludes with a simple reminder that they should contact her – but which is assertive!

You will notice that she does not talk in circles; ideas do not overlap, get mixed up. She is a good business writer! Paragraph 2 deals with technical skills acquired through education and experience. Paragraph 3 deals with human skills, portraying her as a good contact person *for* the company and *in* the company. She also tries to communicate something important she has learned about her personality, i.e., she is productive and yet a team-player!

Her careful use of verbs like 'took part in,' 'developed,' 'taught,' and 'learned' show that she has been learning and is aware of it. Some things we *know*, but first we *learned* them someplace! These verbs show honesty, a certain humility and self-awareness. The impression that is left with the reader is that Marie is a *learner, a grower.* He has no doubt that, once on the job, she will be a self-starter, learn by herself, progress, and learn some more.

Other important words – adjectives and adverbs – communicate a feeling of utility and confidence: 'good position,' 'solid foundation,' 'operational,' 'good contact skills,' 'listen well,' 'valuable information,' 'assertively,' and 'creative and useful suggestions.' She has thought about her personality in depth. Then she has linked her personality with the way she does things. She has learned to characterize everything for greater clarity. This creates a build-up effect that is very powerful.

I have been told that Canon, Inc. is looking for students to conduct surveys about your new photocopier range. I think I am in a good position to apply for this job

A series of courses devoted to marketing research in my Business School have provided me with a solid theoretical foundation for such work. Many class exercises in working up questionnaires, processing statistical data and reporting succinctly on findings have prepared me for both desk research and field work. I also recently took part in a nation-wide survey of French business leaders, which made me operational in conducting business surveys from the exploratory phase to the final report.

◄ Technical Skills

I feel I have developed good contact skills, whether dealing with customers or suppliers. Working in sales brought me in touch with many managers and taught me to listen well to customer problems and get valuable information to report to the home office. Whether as a member of a team, or in the field, I have learned to assertively offer creative and useful suggestions, while maintaining good relations with my co-workers.

◄ 'Soft' or people skills

I have been reading up on developments in the European photocopier market to prepare myself for the opportunity to work for you. I know the competition is tough and that digital technology is reconfiguring the industry. I would like to have the chance to learn more about this industry by carrying through a research project for you.

◄ Interest in the business Learning

I hope to be hearing from you soon.

Yours sincerely,

Marie Taillat

Link the CV and the letter

But we have been looking at the letter alone – as though she didn't send a CV! Actually, for the level of job she is applying, the letter can stand alone effectively. However, she did send a CV, the one on page 223. If we study it, we will notice she did not say the same things again in her letter; she used "the language of skills, self-knowledge, learning and growth" that we mentioned at the beginning. In her letter, she carefully avoids using the same language, even *avoids* giving the same information!

If you put her letter and CV side-by-side you will see the intentional *interplay* between them. The letter, like the house salesman, is constantly pointing at the CV. Marie does this by talking about her experiences as contexts which developed skills, but without names of companies, without places, without details. The reader naturally turns to the CV at each paragraph, perhaps each sentence, to get more information about the context. Thus, he reads both documents completely!

LETTER ➡	**CV**
Marie speaks of Business School.	The recruiter finds the name, place and level of the school.
She mentions a 'nationwide survey'.	The recruiter scans the CV down to Achievements where he finds out the details.
She speaks of 'working in sales' (obviously Business to Business).	The latest work experience as a sales rep suggests Marie has a solid understanding of corporate clients.
She speaks of 'offering creative and useful suggestions'.	The Assembly worker job, which might be unimportant on her CV, suddenly provides a chance to sell this skill.
She refers to 'reporting' twice in her letter.	The reader finds two specific jobs where she 'reported': in accounting and in assembly, besides the 'start-to-finish business survey'.

Marie Taillat
123, rue Victor Hugo
14800 Trouville, France
tel: 33-2-15-49-74-89
mtaillat@email.com

EDUCATION

Currently in Master of Management Program at X School of Management.

1997   Admitted to Master's program on competitive examination, ranking 51out of 3000 candidates.

1995-97   Pre-Business Administration School, Paris, France.

WORK EXPERIENCE

Summer 1999 British Telecom, East Anglia. Colchester, Essex:

> <u>Sales representative</u> in Business Systems Department. Trained in British Telecom selling methods in a two-week course. Assigned to take over from regular in fax machine sales. **Researched prospects, visited several hundreds of firms.** Developed sales approaches to renew regular renew dormant accounts. Negotiated prices and terms of payment. Ranked 4th in the trophy between 50 longstanding representatives and novices.

Summer 1998 Atamer Chemicals, Paris, France

> <u>Accountant:</u> Kept foreign customer and transporter accounts. **Wrote a report** assessing the organization of customer and supplier services.

Summer 1997 SPES cardboard industry, Montreuil, France.

> <u>Assembly worker:</u> Made packages for perfume industry. Noticed and reported waste of time and products due to a bad organization on the assembly line. **Proposed solutions to improve the organization** and the control of quality. Improved productivity rate.

Summer 1996 CL Bank, Chatou, France.

> <u>Counter clerk:</u> Entered customers' deposits and withdrawals ; delivered check books and credit cards. Answered customers' questions about Stock Exchange.

ACHIEVEMENTS

Managed a student polling association : supervised a **start-to-finish business survey** published in the one million-circulation Views magazine; negotiated deadlines with chief editor, worked up the survey questionnaire, briefed 200 pollers, supervised the analysis of the results.

Recruiters often 'jump over' the letter, or are disappointed by it because it seems 'unlinked', 'unrelated' to the CV. They expect the letter to *add* something to the conversation. When your letter fails, either to show genuine interest in the company and its industry, or to strengthen the picture you are trying to build of yourself, then the CV has lost its voice! If your letter seems as though it has nothing to do with the CV, then it seems to the recruiter as though he is interviewing *two* different people at the same time, and he doesn't understand what you want!

Even at a simple level, linking the performance filmed on the CV with 'soft' skills talked about in the letter helps flesh out a three-dimensional picture of the applicant. Take a look at the example below written by a girl who had worked as a teller in a bank:

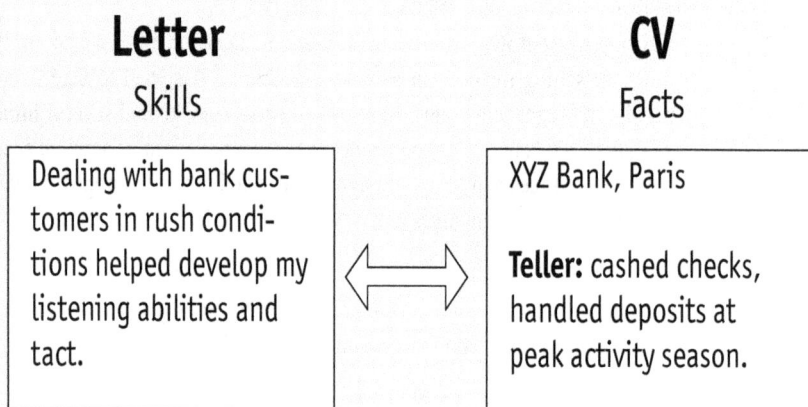

Letter		CV
Skills		Facts
Dealing with bank customers in rush conditions helped develop my listening abilities and tact.	⟸⟹	XYZ Bank, Paris **Teller:** cashed checks, handled deposits at peak activity season.

This link could not have been written by an applicant who had not – beforehand – thought through her skills inventory, placed her skills in situations and then written her job breakdowns. In *playing the movie* she felt it was important to show that she worked during the 'peak activity season', because it was stressful and she handled it well! However, she needs to make that link-up in her letter for the reader, and this allows her to talk about her skills very directly – skills proved by her job breakdown!

On pages 226-227, we see the example of João Reis Oliveira. João has chosen an *Abilities and Achievements* format for his CV. João is a *Career Confirmer* and has great experience in Total Quality Management. He is interested in making a move to general management. Since the *Abilities and Achievements* CV he has chosen stresses technical skills very clearly, in his letter João will try to avoid repetition of the CV and will emphasize his general management capability instead.

Notice how João builds his letter:

In the first paragraph, he goes 'straight to the point' like our other letter writers. He shows knowledge of the company and makes a specific offer of benefits.

In paragraph two, he draws attention rapidly to his *range* of capabilities, rather than repeating them. Expressions like 'solid background', 'all aspects', 'a number of programs', and 'all stages' send the reader's eye over the whole CV. These expressions call for proof – and it is there!

His third paragraph focuses on conceptual, almost strategic skills as well as inter-relational and negotiation skills. He is building on the CV to profit from this interview-like situation where he can sell a high level of knowledge and experience. He reinforces his offer of benefits by labeling precisely what he can bring the company.

Paragraph four moves far beyond the limits of the CV and paints a picture of himself as a high-level learner, ready to make a move into general management. Here the reader finds a skill *which grows out of the accumulation of action verbs and situations*, but which is not contained in any one of them: *leading change!* At the end of his letter, this Quality Manager is selling very clearly his ability to lead a strategic change process.

João Reis Oliveira
8, ave du Général de Gaulle
64200 Biarritz, France
Tel: 33-5-59-17-28
jr-oliveira@email.com

November 17, 1999

Henry Fox
General Manager
UK Motors, Ltd
Manchester, UK

Dear Mr. Fox,

I have read in Industry News about your recent decision to revamp your complete supply and logistics chain for greater reliability and cost effectiveness. I believe I can make a serious contribution to implementing, and then consolidating your new strategy.

My solid background in all aspects of TQM has fully prepared me for an oversight position in carrying through such a major change. I have introduced a number of Quality Management programs for industrial companies, ensuring all stages of the projects from auditing, feasibility studies, budgeting, relationship management, through completion.

My varied experience has provided me with very good insight into the specificities of many industries. This allows me to quickly grasp suppliers' production constraints and negotiate realistic standards and deadlines. Good supplier and customer relationship management has to be founded on understanding of our partners' pressures as well as our market ambitions. I know I can bring my ability in co-designing and partnering in logistics chains to your company.

I read widely in consulting, supply chain management, and outsourcing to stay aware of 'state-of-the-art' developments. Over the years, I have honed my interpersonal skills for carrying through difficult internal changes. You are about to carry through such a major change and will need someone who can win over managers and employees to new ways of working, rather than force it on them.

I will be calling you in about a week to give you more detailed information about myself.

Yours sincerely,

João Reis Oliveira

Encl: CV

João Reis Oliveira
8, ave du Général de Gaulle
64200 Biarritz, France
Tel: 33-5-59-17-28
jr-oliveira@email.com

Job Target: **Quality Control Manager with responsibility for International Supply Chain**

A B I L I T I E S :

- Dealing with suppliers in English at high technical level on specifications, tolerances, ISO certification matters and quality systems.
- Developing and managing relationships with national and international customers
- Planning, setting up and controlling quality control training programs for workers and managers
- Leading full-scale ISO 9000 certification programs, establishing procedure and drafting manuals
- Auditing existing systems and budgeting for TQM changes
- Co-planning with production management plant renewal measures for TQM.

A C H I E V E M E N T S :

- Managed the setting up of an American plant in Portugal. Worked with English, American and German suppliers in English
- Negotiated specifications for refractory bricks with international customers
- Designed and implemented a Computer Integrated Manufacturing system, including tie-ins with suppliers and customers specifications.
- Carried through a complete TQM training program for 200 new employees and management
- Audited suppliers on a monthly basis to maintain quality standards for fast-evolving customer demands
- Produced feasibility and cost-effectiveness studies for top management. Presented findings before Board. Projects adopted.
- Carried through complete ISO 9002 certification program over two years for major industrial glass producer.

W O R K   H I S T O R Y :

1995-99	Lumilux Industrial Glass, Biarritz, France. **TQ Manager**
1993-95	American Canning Corporation, Lisbon, Portugal. **TQ Manager**
1990-93	Lusex Automotive Parts. Sétubal, Portugal. **Quality Supervisor**
1986-90	Evora Brick Company, Sines, Portugal. **Quality Technician**

E D U C A T I O N :

1989-1993	Credits towards a Master's in Industrial Engineering and Management, Instituto Superior Técnico, Lisbon, Portugal.
1986	Instituto de Aveiro, Portugal. Degree in Engineering, major in Quality Control

The closing paragraph

João **ends the letter with** an additional 'knock on the door'. He is interested in the job and will contact them; he is not waiting! He is not a waiter; he is a doer! The last paragraph is very important but may be very short. It should, above all, reaffirm your interest in the job. Saying "I am really interested" is not the way to do it. Here is where the English word *assertiveness* becomes so important. Basically, it means stepping forward and giving your ideas, not being shy. Marie Taillat, above, was a little younger and simply ended by "I hope to be hearing from you soon". João hopes to make a major career move and knows that only positivism will get him there.

The role of the concluding paragraph is not to say good-bye; it is to repeat 'Hello' and your interest in the job, in meeting the person, in having a chance to explain more. In it, you should be straightforward, honest and simple.

Beware of phoniness!

In many of the interviews with recruiters that are printed in this book, you will find constant warnings against lying and phoniness. Phoniness is not the same as lying, but it is being false, not yourself, and therefore not believable. Do

> The worst thing is a 'phony' letter with too much exaggeration on what a great company they think we are. A straightforward statement from the heart is so much more believable.
> **Carolyn Nimmy, Cap Gemini**

not start letters with flattery like "your great company," "your world-famous establishment", and so on. Starting or concluding a letter with flattery or excessive humility just repulses the recruiter. All he or she wants is to see is someone who has something concrete to offer, not a flatterer!

STYLE AND FORM

Content is obviously the most important part of this chapter on letter-writing. Yet, there are a few simple things you should learn about the *form* of an international English letter. You want to draw attention by your content, not by a strange form of letter layout which shocks the reader. After talking about the form, we will make some very important points about style.

Form

The layout of an English language letter

English language letter layouts may vary slightly, but you always do best to stay sober and easily readable. Recruiters always stress that they want it to be easily readable and to find the information fast!

The basic parts of any job application letter are as presented on the following page:

LETTER LAYOUT

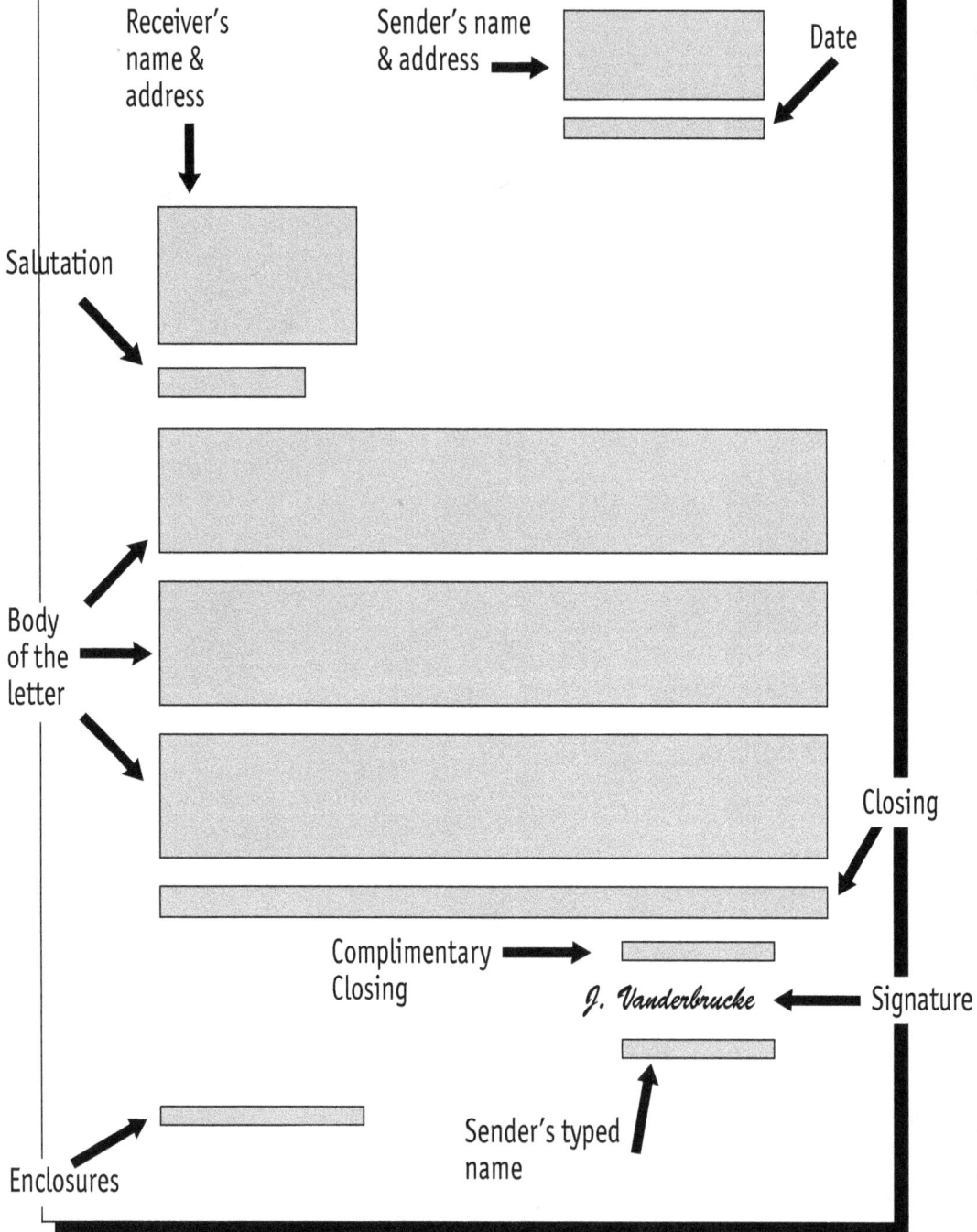

Receiver's name & address

Sender's name & address →

Date

Salutation

Body of the letter →

Closing

Complimentary Closing →

J. Vanderbrucke ← Signature

Sender's typed name

Enclosures

The Letter:
From Top to Bottom

The Sender's name and address (including telephone and e-mail)	Who you are, and where you are writing from or where you want to receive your mail – or your calls
The Date	When you wrote your letter
The Receiver's name and address	Who specifically you want to read your letter and where they work
The Salutation	How you say 'hello' to the receiver/reader
The Body of the letter	Your opening and skills paragraphs, your 'sales arguments'
The Closing	Your reaffirmation of interest in the job and the company
The Complimentary Closing	Your way of saying goodbye in one or two words
Your Signature	Personalizes the letter and shows that it is not a mass mailing circular letter
Your typed name	Under your signature it allows the reader to know who signed that unreadable signature
Enclosures	The abbreviation 'Encl' followed by the words Personal CV or Resume

The layout we have shown you is the one we prefer, because it is personal, rather than machine-like. All information concerning the receiver is on the left, and all information about you, the sender, is on the right. Yet, it is simple and does not wander all over the page! Many companies use in their business correspondence the pure block style layout – shown on the following page – which puts everything but the date on the left. This is a habit which came from the old electric typewriter which sent the carriage automatically back to the left. We find it is more suited to routine communication, rather than a personal first interview. Choose whichever suits you best, but keep it readable!

Block style layout

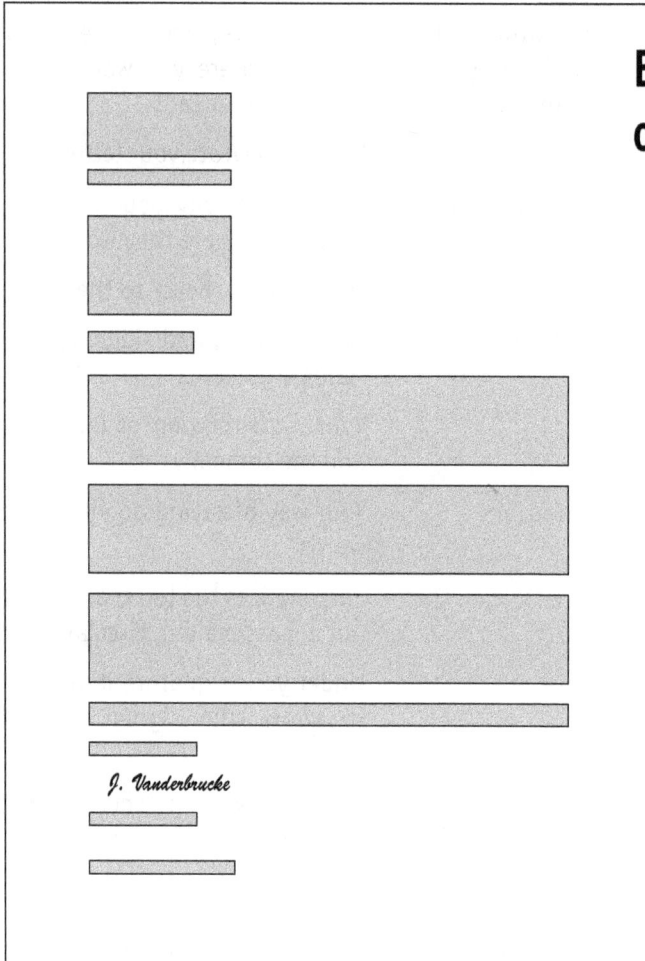

Everything on the left!

J. Vanderbrucke

The Sender's name and address

You name should be at the top before the address and retyped at the bottom of the letter as well. This is because you always introduce yourself before talking. You also want the recruiter to know who is talking to him from the very beginning. At the bottom it serves as both a reminder and a polite clarification of your signature.

In English we have first names, middle names and last names. The British refer to these as Christian names, middle names and surnames. On more and more international documents, the word 'family name' is being used for the last, or 'sur', name. Whatever the nomenclature, in English:

• The first name goes first.
• The middle names goes in the middle – if you have one and use it!
• The last name goes last.

We include the telephone number, and e-mail, as part of the address – obviously you can be contacted there! When writing internationally for jobs, you should include the country code for your telephone number, as did João Reis Oliveira below. Some applicants feel it is better to put their telephone number at the bottom of the letter, right below their typed name, as if to say "call me" at the end of the letter. There is also good logic in this.

It should be remembered that, whereas in some countries, the city is written all in capitals, English writers rarely capitalize the name of either the city or country. Everything is very sober. João's way of doing this is the same on his CV and on his letter:

> João Reis Oliveira
> 8, ave du Général de Gaulle
> 64200 Biarritz, France
> Tel: 33-5-59-17-28
> jr-oliveira@email.com

More and more often, individuals, like companies, will make their own letterhead stationery. They may place their name and address in the center top or side top, almost like a kind of logo. If you do so, make sure it is readable! *Avoid stylized or fancy print* that might be found on personal stationery or very special effects, like the examples below, unless you are in advertising:

Do these look 'businesslike?'

João Reis Oliveira
8, ave du Général de Gaulle
64200 Biarritz, France

João Reis Oliveira
8, ave du Général de Gaulle
64200 Biarritz, France

The date

This needs no explanation, but remember not to write just figures. When you write a CV or a letter, you are not filling out a form for a driver's license. Type the month out and capitalize the first letter. It is becoming less important in international business whether the month goes first or second, but it helps the reader feel the letter is personal when he can read the date easily, without going into mathematics. With figures, depending on the country, you are not always sure if 7/11 is July 11th or the 7th of November.

This is clear and personal	This is ugly and not clear
November 7, 1999 7 November 1999 7th November 1999	7/11/99 11/7/99

The receiver's name and address

Remember to put the name of the person addressed first and his or her title second, before the actual mailing address. Make every effort to *find out the name of the person you are writing to*, the full name! Letters written to companies, if they are ever read, show a lack of interest by the applicant who did not phone, write or e-mail in order to find out who to write to. Letters written to titles, like Human Resource Manager, are a little better, but do not show that extra involvement and caring that they are expecting. Just remember when you get your mail in the morning, you will always read the mail addressed to you personally first – not the mail that says "Dear Homeowner" or "Resident". Such mail is just 'bumph' or 'junk mail' and finds its way quickly to the trash! In the example below, Henry Fox may actually receive and read the beginning of the letter at least!

Henry Fox
General Manager
UK Motors, Ltd.
Manchester, UK

Knowing the full name is important for another reason. It keeps you from writing to <u>Mrs</u>. Fox, when actually the General Manager, in this case, is a man! Yet, it is not that simple. When communicating between countries, first names that are men's in one country may be women's in another. For example, Jean is a man's name in France and a woman's in England or the US, whereas Gene (pronounced like Jean) is a man in English-speaking countries. Leslie, or Lesley, may be either a man or woman. Other languages, like Hungarian or Finnish, may have names that people further West may have difficulty attaching genders to. Therefore, when you go international, it may be difficult to determine whether you, the applicant, are a man or woman, or whether the person you are writing to is a man or woman. In a sense, this might be good, because it helps prevent sexual discrimination!

However, when writing to someone, it is preferable not to write to a woman as Mr. – or to a man as Mrs.

Salutations

It is important to know how to address someone in an international English context – and it is very simple.

Mr.	Is used before the last name of any man
Mrs.	Is used before the last name of any woman who has personally – through correspondence or in conversation – mentioned that she is married.
Ms. (pronounced Mizz)	Before the last name of **any woman in a professional context** you do not know to be married or single.
Miss	**Never used** in written form unless the woman asks for it.

If you write to Henry Fox, as above, you will address the letter to him and his title, and then start your letter with:

Dear Mr. Fox,

In English speaking contexts, "Dear Mr., Dear Mrs. or Dear Ms…" is the rule. Never forget the "Dear". To forget it would be impolite! If you write to a manager without knowing his or her name, use "Dear Sir" in all cases. "Dear Sirs", or in American, "Gentlemen" is used when you write to a company in general. But, remember, letters sent to companies in general wind up in the trash can. You should always write to "Dear Mr." or "Dear Ms." *somebody*, because you have done your homework on the company and its managers and found out their names!

Body of the letter and the Closing

We have talked a lot about this from the point of view of content. All we need to add here are issues of typing: **indentation and spacing**. Do you indent paragraphs – that is, start the first line further away from the margin than the rest of the paragraph? Do you double space between lines, between paragraphs, etc.? The rules are simple good sense:

Most modern letters are single-spaced within paragraphs and double-spaced between paragraphs, as are most of the examples in this book. There are reasons for this: single-spacing gives you more room to talk without going on to a second page; and double-spacing between paragraphs separates your ideas into nice, easy-to-see batches, as below:

My solid background in all aspects of TQM has fully prepared me for an oversight position in carrying through such a major change. I have introduced a number of Quality Management programs for industrial companies, ensuring all stages of the projects from auditing, feasibility studies, budgeting, relationship management, through completion.

My varied experience has provided me with very good insight into the specificities of many industries. This allows me to quickly grasp suppliers' production constraints and negotiate realistic standards and deadlines. Good supplier and customer relationship management has to be founded on understanding of our partners' pressures as well as our market ambitions. I know I can bring my ability in co-designing and partnering in logistics chains to your company.

Both indenting paragraphs and double spacing between them seems an unnecessary complication and may make the letter less easy to read. However, it doesn't really matter, as long as paragraphs are separated into easy-to-access central ideas.

The Complimentary Closing

There are many forms of complimentary closing, but for our purposes, just one: "Yours sincerely", or "Sincerely". You will find many books that explain all the different forms of address and salutations for business correspondence. In Great Britain, it is often advised to use "Yours faithfully" when you write to a company or to a title. That's fine, but you are going to write to a person with a name. So you will sign:

> **Yours sincerely,**
>
> **OR**
>
> **Sincerely,**

Your signature

This needs no further comment. *Just remember to sign above your typed name.*

Your typed name

Type your name just under the complimentary closing, but about four lines below it to leave room for your signature. Remember, unlike in some cultures, none of these names are capitalized.

Enclosures

All you need to do to show that you have included a CV or Resume is type **"Encl: Personal CV" or "Encl: Personal Resume"** at the bottom of your letter. This should be typed about two lines below your name and on the left.

Last points on Layout

The letter: handwritten or typed?

Here we come back to the question of whether the letter should be typed or handwritten. We dealt with this in some detail in Chapter Two. However, a short reminder: In across border job applications, you should normally *type* both the letter and the CV. International business is carried out by typing! Internet applications are obviously imposing the need to type everything! *Handwrite your letter only when it is requested in the advertisement.*

Should you put a "Subject" heading on your letter?

The answer is clearly no. You might well put an *Objective* or *Job Target* heading on your CV, but on a letter "Subject" is only used in routine and very formal correspondence between companies. Your letter is a personal "Hello" and sales offer. Let the recruiter read the first paragraph to find out the subject!

Style

There are enough examples in this book to give you a good idea about writing style. Second, style is a very personal thing, and recruiters hire individuals, not robots. However, if we can make a few suggestions they would be this:

1. 'Talk' naturally

2. Be very direct

3. Don't use useless words or connectives

4. Use an active prose, not a passive prose.

'Talk' naturally

Do not become a different person when you write than when you talk! The letter is your chance to have that first conversation with the recruiter. It is not a school dissertation nor a poem – unless you naturally write poetically. Too often, our seminar participants tend to lecture or teach in their letters. They want to show off a lot of knowledge about the industry they want to work in and so they build into their letters a paragraph that sounds like it was taken out of a business magazine. This bores the reader. Do not forget the recruiter wants to find out about you – not the industry in which he works! So always link knowledge you may have with yourself as a person and the offer you are making. Remember that Marie Taillat showed some of her knowledge of the photocopier market, but she never made a wide detour, *she always linked this knowledge with what she wanted to do as a person.*

I have been reading up on developments in the European photocopier market <u>to prepare myself for the opportunity to work</u> for you. I know the competition is tough and that digital technology is reconfiguring the industry. <u>I would like to have the chance to learn more about this industry</u> by carrying through a research project for you.

Never "beat about the bush". Do not think you will get the reader's attention by getting him involved as if your letter were a mystery novel. Remember the lessons in Chapter Two. In essence, tell the reader what you want, why you want it and why you should get it. Just remember the lessons we have learned about quoting precise facts, data, and events that prove that you have the skills you are offering.

"Beating about the bush" often happens because we use expressions we find in books, but which do not really suit what we want to say. This particularly happens if English is not our native tongue. Typical examples are: "I look forward to hearing from you soon", or "Don't hesitate to ask me for further information". *These expressions are common English expressions, but do not belong in a cover letter to ask for a job.* They even seem arrogant at the end of such a letter! Wouldn't you frankly prefer to say "Please contact me soon for more information," or "I can provide a more detailed CV of my experience and skills whenever you wish".

Once again: just talk naturally to the recruiter!

Don't use useless words or connectives

Many letter writers, who indeed forget how to talk when they write, fill a letter up with a lot of words, instead of real ideas. Adjectives are useful when they add something important. Indeed, an <u>adjective</u> should <u>add</u>! Use them when they clarify a skill or a result, but use just enough.

Connectives like "and, as well as, but" are useful when writing and direct. However, many people feel that they need to guide the reader through their logic like an argument. Such writers fall back on expressions like: 'moreover', 'besides', 'therefore', 'thus', etc. These are fine for school dissertations, but are poor in a sales talk. The logic of your letter will be evident, if you have thought it out carefully before. Sentences like: "I have studied marketing for two years, therefore I can work in your marketing department" are tragic. First of all, this is deductive logic, not empirical proof! 'Therefore' always sounds as if you are trying to trick somebody to fall into a trap. It would be far better to make a link-up that is based on fact and a degree of positivism. Take a look at the example below:

Unbelievable	**Credible**
I have studied market-ing for two years, <u>therefore</u> I can work in your marketing depart-ment	Two years of studying marketing at school have given me a solid foundation for tackling an operational marketing job.

How many of us would really sit down in front of an interviewer and say: "I did this, therefore I can do this"? Almost any of us would more naturally say: "My experience on that job prepared me to do this for you!"

Use an active prose, not a passive prose

In the second sentence, on the right, the applicant has written a much more active prose and presented a more convincing picture. He is selling! His sentence is just as direct as if he had said, like a lawnmower salesman "this powerful motor will make it easy to mow lawns over 1500 square meters". Essentially, in the second sentence, the applicant has gone back to the flowchart sentence structure we studied in Chapter Four. The flowchart sentence structure that we used in our job breakdowns works very well here and guides the reader quickly through a series of factual events that lead to results. It reads dynamically and suggests energy!

WHAT NOT TO SAY

There are some subjects that are better left to the interview and not mentioned in a letter. They are more or less obvious: anything that shows possible disadvantages to hiring you. These are salary requirements, relocation expenses, your husband's or wife's career, and starting dates for the job. Your objective is to get the interview. When they really like you, then you can approach subjects that might seem negative if they are up front. If you are looking for an internship, and they want you to work at the wrong times, the starting dates can be negotiated later. If you are going to put in information about when you can work, always put it positively, like: "I will be ready to start work as of July 1st".

INTERVIEW # 9
WRITE A LETTER THAT SELLS BENEFITS !

Interview with Margarida Faustino, Human Resources Manager at Johnson & Johnson LDA, Portugal.

▶ **What do you expect from applicants at Johnson & Johnson?**

We expect people to be aware of the company culture and, most of all, of "Our Credo Document." We don't like to be treated like one of the many recipients of a circular letter. The person who talks to us, knows something about us, really wants to work with us has a definite advantage. That interest can be shown in many ways, but it takes homework. One example was a person who wrote a CV applying for a medical detailing position in the form of a medical prescription. It was obviously meant for us, and, although original, was not gratuitously original. He was also able to identify the skills that this position meant for our company. This showed he wanted to grow in the company, evolve and learn, and that he understood the scope of that particular position.

▶ **What are some of the values you seek in your recruits?**

I would say the main ones are: *Customer orientation, integrity, innovation, creativity, the capacity to link things together* and *open-mindedness*.
Integrity is essential, since we hope to be working with the person for some time. We don't believe integrity comes with age, so whether the candidate is 20 or 50, it is important.

242

Innovation, creativity and the capacity to link things together are important skills, because we want people with long-term potential that can be developed. We hope to help people grow, so open-mindedness is important as well.

▶ What kind of CVs do you prefer?

A CV is a first identity, a commercial link between us and the candidate. We expect the candidate to sell benefits clearly, to make the link-up between our expectations and what he or she is offering. However, this kind of clear-cut view is very rare. Most applicants tend to send applications to just anybody. Such applications fail to speak to us specifically. Applicants should know where they are going when they write a CV. They should know themselves. For example, a candidate makes it much easier if he knows, and says, he does not like finance, does not like figures. He has saved everybody a lot of time. We are becoming less and less patient with people who do not know where they are going, and apply to anybody with a kind of standard offer.

We have no preference for any particular structure in a CV. The simpler, the more legible, the better. We prefer our CVs in English, as not everybody here speaks Portuguese. Above all, for us to shortlist a candidate the CV has to make a difference. When we read 150 CVs and nothing tells us specifically why we should interview such and such a person, it is very frustrating. We cannot waste time on people who did not spend time asking themselves what they had to offer that we wanted!

▶ Could you describe what you consider to be a good cover letter?

The letter has to be specifically intended for Johnson & Johnson, not be a standardized letter sent to everybody. It has to be human and be truthful. I must confess that only one in a thousand applicants manages to write a letter that is linked to the CV, so we have stopped expecting them to be able to do it! But they should...

▶ Do you have some advice to give candidates about the interview?

Yes. Sleep well before the interview, eat well, do not show up all shaky. Being nervous does not help; it keeps you from being yourself – and we want to see who you really are! Don't lie; it shows immediately. Before you come, do your homework, know what your customer (us) wants. Don't fire all your guns; just sell benefits! Sell your benefits to the customer, just the things he is looking for. This means, once again, that you have to know what he is looking for.

An example of this: we were looking for somebody young for a new product we were developing. We wanted somebody who could grow into the position and make that position grow as well. It was very important that the person interviewed had already put himself or herself 'into our shoes' before the interview and knew the skills we were looking for, was sensitive enough to understand what we needed. In the end, the successful candidate knew what benefits to sell. The person we hired knew he would have to train other people. He explained he liked to teach, he had done some teaching in the past and was proud of it, had really enjoyed it. That's what I mean by selling benefits!

Key points in chapter seven

- The letter is a sales talk.

- Tell the recruiter what you know about his company and what you want in the very first paragraph.

- In the rest of the letter talk about your skills.

- Link the letter to the CV closely.

- End your letter with another 'knock on the door'.

- Do not be phony.

- Use English letter layout.

- Just talk to the recruiter as if he were in front of you.

- Write active, not passive prose.

- Dans la lettre vous devez vous montrer vendeur.

- Dans le premier paragraphe, expliquez brièvement ce que vous savez de l'entreprise et ce qui vous y attire, ce que vous en attendez : type de poste, stage/emploi...

- Le reste de la lettre porte sur vos compétences.

- Etablissez un lien clair entre le CV et la lettre.

- En fin de lettre, n'hésitez pas à "retaper à la porte".

- Ne soyez pas faux, ne soyez pas hypocrite.

- Utilisez un format de lettre anglo-saxon.

- Parlez au recruteur comme s'il se trouvait devant vous.

- Ecrivez de manière active et n'utilisez pas de prose inutile ou passive.

Applying to MBA Programs

We felt this short chapter was a needed add-on in a book on CV-writing. In the world of life-long learning we are now living in, whether we consider ourselves career starters, career changers or career confirmers, we may decide to go back to school for our learning. Many of the participants in our CV-writing courses decide to apply to MBA programs, sometimes right after graduation, but often after some years of professional work. The application forms of American or European MBA programs almost always require a CV or Resume, as well as a series of essays or papers on applicants' backgrounds, personalities and career goals.

A CARRY-OVER FROM CV-WRITING

What you have learned in this book can be directly carried over to the writing of applications to graduate school, whether for MBA or M.Sc. programs. You will be asked to write essays that show a high degree of self-knowledge. You will be expected to analyze past experience and show what you have learned about performance and yourself through this experience. Your leadership and relational skills will be probed. Typical questions might run like this:

- Describe activities in which you are involved or have been involved and your role in them.
- Describe leadership positions you have held and what you did.
- Provide a candid description of yourself, your strengths and weaknesses. Give examples when possible.
- What main factors or events have influenced your personal development?

- What have been some of your main accomplishments? Why do you consider them important?

- Describe a personal setback, how it affected you and what you learned.

- What would others say about you as a team member and leader? Why?

- What are your career goals and how will our MBA program contribute to them?

INTERVIEW # 10
WHAT SHOULD BE SHOWN IN AN MBA APPLICATION

Interview with Mary Clark, Assistant Director for Recruitment, IESE, Spain.

▶ **Can you explain in general the IESE MBA recruiting process?**

IESE is the International Graduate School of Management of the University of Navarra, with campuses in Barcelona and Madrid. IESE is dedicated to the education of international managers through its MBA Program. The MBA is taught in both English and Spanish. We have very diverse recruitment objectives, because we want a varied and interesting student body from General Management schools, Science and Engineering schools, etc. Our age group average is 28 with people ranging in age from 23 to 35. We seek diversity in terms of nationality and cultural background, academic and professional experience. What they will all have in common is that they have demonstrated leadership abilities.

We have a long and complete application process, as the applicants are expected to reflect on why they want to join our program, what they have done in the past, where their interests and their potentials lie. We follow up the written application with a personal interview which lasts from one to one and a half hours. A very important part of the written application, besides the CV, is applicants' essays. In these essays, we ask them to talk about work experience, professional and other qualifications, and their personality features.

▶ What does IESE look for in MBA applicants' written papers?

Through these essays, we probe candidates' activities, leadership qualities, career plans and their self-awareness concerning success, failure and their skills. Through this writing, we want to confirm that the applicant has been a leader, taken responsibility – launched or led a student club or activity, taken responsibility for employees, made changes or introduced innovations in his/her company or environment, has already been in a management position, etc. The candidate's description will serve as a good indicator of leadership potential for the future. If the essays do not match reality, or if the reality was embellished, we will usually find that out during the interview.

The essays are crucial, as they are one of the few opportunities candidates have to communicate to the Admissions committee what they are about. We recognize that some people are not good writers. In that case, they should get some help from people who know how to write, but without compromising the content of their essays.

We will typically ask candidates to talk about their accomplishments and failures. This helps us find out really what kind of person we are dealing with. For example, when the person says he or she has had no failures, we know that they have not thought about the subject enough, or they lack humility or depth. This statement says a lot about the person's attitude.

▶ What are the most common difficulties applicants face in writing these papers?

Above all, self-knowledge. It is an essential part of the admissions process. As they are only allowed a certain number of words, they need to be precise. Thus, they really have to sort things out. To be clear, they need to spend time reflecting, organizing, and prioritizing; some people do have trouble with this! Those who do not spend enough time analyzing their progress and their objectives, suffer. Prioritizing is the key: through the writing we see what the candidate felt was essential. The space allotted limits the candidate and forces him or her to a greater clarity of view.

What links all of these questions is self-analysis and self-awareness! Whether you apply to a post-experience MBA, after several years of work experience, or to an MBA program right after graduation, you will be asked to run through the same process we have run through together in Chapters Three and Four. And you will have to prioritize as in Chapter Five. The only difference is that the schools' applications will allow you a little more space to talk about your experience than is allowed by the one-page CV.

To a large extent, writing answers to questions like those we have listed above requires that you blend together the CV and letter! Let's go back to our young graduate in Chapter Three who drew up the following skills inventory for himself:

✔ Playing as a team member
✔ Acting tactfully
✔ Being thought of as highly reliable and taking on new responsibilities
✔ Building on others' ideas
✔ Originating ideas
✔ Seeing the value in older ways of doing things
✔ Anticipating reactions of people and sensing whether they will support a proposal
✔ Showing patience with difficult or demanding people
✔ Picking up on people's feelings, reactions, and attitudes

You will remember he had also worked out that his main skill, that summarized the effect of these other skills, was:

Growing quickly into an effective team member

At the time he wrote that, he was applying for jobs that would take him abroad with companies setting up operations in other countries, and he wanted to stress how quickly he would fit in. On his CV he would undoubtedly show situations in which he had developed and applied this skill. Now, however, he has decided to go on to further study and needs to write a *personal statement* about himself. He will take one or two situations, play a movie of himself acting and learning in these situations and write a Letter/CV combination for the MBA application. He will be describing a process of self-discovery! Here, he is answering the question:

"Describe an event in which you learned a great deal about yourself as a leader."

I remember my first internship with a production company during a tense restructuring period. Sales had fallen off over the previous two years and productivity was poor. New automation was being brought in and some employees were going to be laid off. I had landed an internship period with the company, and, because of my education, I was assigned to carry through a study of the best ways of setting up the new production process and then report my findings to plant management. I was given a free hand, but I knew the situation was a delicate one. My superiors were very demanding, short on time and temper, and, I felt, considered me more a burden than a help. I requested permission to run a few workers' meetings to collect ideas and gain support for changes. This was granted.

In these meetings, I was looked upon with suspicion both because of my university education and my relations with management. I managed to get the workers to participate in a kind of 'quality circles' to contribute ideas on how best to use the new integrated manufacturing system. Over a period of two months, I managed to gain their confidence and proved to them that my only interest was to use their expertise to help carry through the changes. Management became aware that I was helping the atmosphere and gathering useful ideas from the shop floor.

Through this experience, I realized that I was able to learn a great deal from others through listening and quickly become accepted as one of the group by getting seriously involved in projects of common interest. I was also able to contribute original ideas and convince people of their value. The experience also taught me to overcome resistance from higher levels by using facts and logical argument rather than emotion.

This experience was one of several which made me realize that I had leadership ability and made me sure I wanted to move into management. For this I need to do an MBA program to gain a greater overview of the factors coming into play in companies' evolution, understand better what motivates men and women in organizations, and learn to think more like a manager. I also realized I needed far greater knowledge of production planning and operations, which your school stresses in its curriculum.

Notice how he has essentially written a kind of job breakdown, but in longer form, sensitive to the importance of showing the context, so that he can clearly communicate the skills he had already inventoried. The *movie* has to be clear if the admissions committee is to understand his skills and potential as a future manager. He has blended with it the kind of commentary you might write in a letter. He finishes with an explanation of why he is attracted by the school he is writing to. And he did it in about 30 lines – which is what the school stipulated!

BRINGING IN THE LONG-TERM FUTURE

MBA applications often add questions about your long-term career goals. This is no different from what a recruiter expects to hear from you in a letter or, at least, in the interview. Above all, both recruiters and MBA admissions committees expect to see some coherence between your past and your future. They do not expect to see this in rigid terms of having a lot of experience in finance and wanting to go into finance. Rather they expect some growing awareness through experiences in your past that you would like and be suited to a certain kind of future.

Key points in chapter eight

- In applying to an MBA program show self-awareness.

- Draw on past experience to show skills just like in a CV.

- Make the link between what you have learned about yourself and your future career.

- Lorsque vous postulez pour un MBA, montrez que vous avez bien compris et analysé les raisons de votre choix.

- Utilisez vos expériences passées pour faire valoir vos compétences, comme dans un CV.

- Faites le lien entre ce que vous avez appris sur vous-même et votre carrière à venir.

A few last words

S ince the time this book was written, a certain number of events have taken place that make the message of the book even more relevant to the new context. What are these events? They are:

- A boom in management education.
- A new focus on managerial skills.
- An increase in the use of Internet as a recruiting tool.
- Greater across-border job mobility in Europe and the world.

THE BOOM IN MANAGEMENT EDUCATION

A few years ago, the MBA degree was predominantly an American or UK degree and was just beginning to make its appearance on the European continent. Since then, the European educational scene has changed considerably. MBA-type programs have more than doubled in number in France and Germany, and they are spreading to Northern and Central Europe. MBA Fairs are held all over the world to recruit international students for European programs. In order to be truly international programs with an international student body, these programs are taught in English, and their graduates are trained to apply for jobs with English CVs. The number of job seekers writing a CV in English has increased greatly.

THE NEW FOCUS ON MANAGERIAL SKILLS

Associated with the boom in management education, has been greater awareness of the need to develop managerial skills. By managerial skills, we do not mean technical skills–like engineering or finance–we mean primarily "people" skills, the ability to work with others in the most productive fashion, quickly creating good relationships, communicating easily, gaining support from others and leading projects to good results, influencing creativity. These are the main skills stressed in Chapters 3 and 4 of this book.

Nowadays, many schools in the US and Europe have launched courses to develop abilities such as team-building, leadership, and creativity. Recruiters are aware that graduates have been trained in these areas, both on the job and at school. For you, this means that it is more important than ever to be able to communicate something clearly about your skills to recruiters who are looking for these skills from applicants–and expecting to find them!

AN INCREASED USE OF INTERNET IN RECRUITING

The great majority of firms have Internet sites with pages devoted to *Careers*. Careers-linked pages will often include sections on *View Jobs, Apply on line*, and often a section like *Recruiting Philosophy*. Using Internet correctly in job-seeking still means "finding out about the company", as we described in Chapter 3. Internet just makes it easier. Firms spell out clearly the kinds of people they want, their value systems and the careers open to you. This information should be read carefully, and careful self-analysis should be carried through before filling out an application on line.

Often you will be asked to "paste" a CV into a box on the application site. This means that careful preparation and drafting of a CV is just as important as before. Letters are not always asked for–this means that your CV must somehow say everything you want it to! However, in place of the letter, you will often be asked to go through a rather complete questionnaire, which mixes factual information, such as education, with questions concerning the kind of person you are. Questions are similar to some of those we have seen in this book and will stress, above all, *self-knowledge*. These questions play the role of a first interview, trying to find out about your initiative, leadership, commitment, etc.

To prepare for these questionnaires or on-line tests, go through the thinking process you would go through to write a paper CV and letter *before* you apply on line. Force yourself to write your paper CV and letter. Don't worry about being "trapped" into saying something you don't wish to; most sites allow you to update your application. The companies want you to study their values, know the company, and know yourself well. They want you to prepare and help them make the "fit".

INCREASED ACROSS-BORDER JOB MOBILITY

The last major event–or perhaps process–that needs to be pointed out is the increased mobility of people across borders, particularly in Europe. The European Union is making itself felt, perhaps most through the mobility of firms that are becoming more transnational. As once national firms are becoming more European or global, they recruit a wider spectrum of personnel and move their employees from country to country more often. Knowing that it is very likely that their employees will be asked to relocate, they look for *international* people in their recruiting; they look for people who demonstrate openness of mind, confidence, self-starter ability and, above all, once again, "people" skills. The latter are very necessary when working with different cultures and in changing contexts.

Much of this mobility is taking place among student populations, made possible by student exchange and study abroad programs. If you are a younger applicant, make sure to stress your participation in such programs. A period abroad is often perceived as the best part of your education.

Educational systems are also "going international". Slowly but certainly, European educational systems are converging. This means that you don't need to worry about communicating your education to a recruiter in another country. Make it clear and brief as shown in Chapter 5, and move on to those aspect that show what kind of person you are.

In conclusion, the events mentioned above have made it even more necessary than before for job-seekers to work on their knowledge of themselves, be aware of their personal development, have a future in mind and to be able to communicate that knowledge, that development and that future.

Conclusion

YOU'VE BEEN CALLED TO THE INTERVIEW, WHAT NOW?

On your long journey through your 'self', what kind of person you are to work with, what you have done and what you can do, you have learned to write a letter and CV that communicates some very important things about you that the recruiter wants to know. Your letter and CV have succeeded in getting you called to an interview. When you get the phone call or the letter calling you to the interview, this is not the time to break out the champagne. Do not just lay back and relax – continue preparing! Do not make the mistake of thinking you have won the game!

Many people make the mistake of betting everything on the CV and feel when they are contacted that the interview is just a formality. This is far from the truth. You have been 'shortlisted', true, but you are still in competition with others who have also been called to the interview. There is no doubt that you have overcome an important hurdle: your application did not go into the trash; you *did* say something that interested the recruiter. On the other hand, you do not know the competition and you do not know if you are at the top of the pile or at the bottom. In other words, you do not know if you are walking into the interview as the recruiter's first choice, or one among many!

Your best attitude now is not to worry about the competition, because you cannot do anything about them. Focus on understanding what the interviewer wants to learn from the interview-and once again – what you have to offer!

WHAT DOES THE INTERVIEWER WANT FROM THE INTERVIEW?

You understand interviews pretty well. After all, you have written your CV as a 'pre-interview' after very careful reflection and structuring. The problem is that you may not know, despite careful preparation, what exactly in your letter and CV attracted the company's attention. Yet, since you built your CV and letter intelligently, planned what accomplishments, skills and benefits should show up in your application package, it is not a total mystery either. Now it is time to sit down and read over your own letter and CV again. Read through your application like a recruiter. Imagine yourself setting your own CV aside in the «to be interviewed» pile. Imagine yourself, like the recruiter, on a busy day, preparing to interview one or many of the candidates he has pre-selected for an interview. What does he want to find out during that interview? And what is the link between the CV you have written and the interview questions he will ask?

Remember that the interview has a variety of purposes: *confirming, deepening, and challenging*.

- First the interviewer will want to *confirm* his first impression of you. He will seek proof to reinforce, strengthen, and assure himself that the first impression was founded. He will want to prove he was right about you, that you have value. At the same time, he is going to meet others and will want to prove that he was right about them too.

- Once reassured that he was right to 'listen' to your CV, he is going to probe for information that will provide a fuller, *deeper* picture of your skills and readiness for the job, and, most of all, your potential for growth. Now he will want you to 'play many movies' in your mind that show you using a variety of secondary skills related to the job. Even if you have studied a job description or completely researched the functions involved in the position, the chances are that you will not have a similar experience to pull out for every question. The best strategy to adopt in this situation is honest dialogue, dialogue about your potential for learning and realism about a lack of experience.

- Thirdly, he will seek some 'contrary evidence', that is, evidence that *challenges* his first impression. He knows that nobody is perfect.

Many recruiters use 'contrary evidence' either explicitly or implicitly. It is an approach based on the common sense conclusion that you have made mistakes, that you have not always acted the way the situation required. Thus, the trained interviewer will probe for examples of your mistakes and expect information about them. This contrary evidence will help him separate the true individual from the 'bluffer', the 'phony'.

USE YOUR CV TO PREPARE FOR THE INTERVIEW

Above all, think of the interview as an occasion where the recruiter will give you even more time to show the company why they should want you on their team. But he will expect you to have 'pre-digested' and 'pre-planned' your message, showing that you have understood his business needs.

Review the message you tried to convey in your letter and CV, so that you can support it in a face-to-face interview even more solidly with real-life examples and more detail about what you have learned through your experience. You must think more deeply about what you have to offer the company if you start to work with them *tomorrow*. Above all, focus on the learning you have gone through, remembering that companies hire people who can keep on learning, growing with them. Build your case on complete self-knowledge and go to the interview self-assured and ready to be thoughtful and truthful.

DURING THE INTERVIEW

Do not play a role you cannot carry! Later you will be unhappy with the company if you do. At the interview, you will be nervous, so admit it. It may help relax the atmosphere and create an attitude of mutual information seeking and providing. Consider the interview a problem that both you and the recruiter are working on together to solve. You are both seeking and providing information to reach that goal. It is natural for you to ask questions about the company, the challenges you will face and the opportunities you will have to progress with the company. If you do not know the answer to a question or have never faced a certain situation, admit it and try to learn about it.

The management logic that runs through this book should accompany you to the interview. Go as a problem-solver, show your capabilities in solving some problems and your ability to learn how to solve the others.

Glossary
English French

Account for	*Rendre compte de, expliquer*
Achieve	*Réaliser*
Act on hunches	*Suivre ses intuitions*
Ascertain	*Vérifier, déterminer*
Assertive	*Assuré, sûr de soi*
Assertively	*De manière sûre*
Assess	*Évaluer*
Attain	*Atteindre*
Back up	*Défendre, soutenir*
Balance	*Équilibrer*
Bounce it off a friend	*Le tester sur un ami*
Brag	*Se vanter*
Bring (brought) about	*Provoquer*
Bumph (junk mail)	*Paperasse*
Buzzwords	*Mots à la mode*
Chart	*Retracer*
Cog in a machine	*Etre un simple rouage dans une machine*
Colon	*Deux points*
Comma	*Virgule*
Compound	*Composer, transiger*
Cost (costed)	*Évaluer le coût, établir un devis*
Counsel	*Conseiller*
Critique (critiqued)	*Faire une critique positive, apprécier(une situation)*
Cutting through red tape	*Prendre un raccourci, accélérer un processus (administratif lent)*
Defuse	*Désamorcer*
Demotion	*Etre rétrogradé*
Department managers	*Responsables de rayon, de service*
Desktop publishing documents	*Des documents PAO*
Dislike	*Aversion,*
Dispense	*Distribuer, prodiguer*
Doers	*'Faiseurs', acteurs*
Draft	*Rédiger*
Draw up (drew up)	*Rédiger*
Engineer (engineered)	*Faire de l'ingénierie (financière, etc), organiser un projet*
Effusive	*Démonstratif, expansif*
Embellishment	*Embellissement*
File (filed)	*Classer des documents*

Fishbone chart	*Graphique en arête de poisson*
Found (founded)	*Créer, fonder*
Flesh out	*Donner du relief*
Fundraising drive	*Campagne pour la taxe d'apprentissage ou pour lever des fonds*
Gather	*Rassembler*
Handle	*Manipuler, s'occuper de*
Head (headed)	*Diriger*
Hire	*Embaucher*
Home in on	*Se diriger vers, focaliser sur*
Indentation	*Alinéa*
Internship	*Stage (en américain)*
Inverted commas	*Guillemets*
Job breakdown	*Analyse d'un métier, d'une fonction*
Junk mail	*Prospectus postaux*
Keying in data	*Saisir des données*
Lecture (lectured)	*Donner une conférence, faire cours*
Leeway	*Marge de manœuvre*
Legibility, readability	*Compréhension, lisibilité*
Log (logged)	*Enregistrer, faire des écritures comptables*
Make ends meet	*Joindre les deux bouts*
Mastermind	*Piloter*
Meandering	*Sinueux, mal organisé, peu synthétique*
Mediate	*Servir d'intermédiaire dans des négociations*
Mess/es	*Situation(s) chaotique(s)*
Monitor	*Superviser, contrôler*
Numbercrunching	*Calcul*
Outcomes	*Résultats, réalisations*
Overcome	*Surmonter*
Overhaul	*Remanier, restructurer*
Oversee (oversaw)	*Superviser, chapeauter*
Performance appraisal	*Evaluation des résultats*
Perform	*Exécuter, effectuer*
Phone-canvass (phone-canvassed)	*Faire du démarchage téléphonique*
Phoniness	*Hypocrisie*
Phony	*Factice, faux, hypocrite, mensonger*
Pinned down	*Bien cerné*
Prevent	*Empêcher*
Provide	*Fournir*

Purchase	*Acheter*
Puffed up	*Gonflé d'orgueil*
Quotation marks	*Guillemets*
Raising funding	*Collecter des fonds*
Rapport (building rapport)	*Rapport (établir un rapport entre vous et quelqu'un), établir une relation avec quelqu'un, 'lire' l'autre*
Record	*Enregistrer, noter*
Refer to	*Rendre compte à quelqu'un*
Refine	*Peaufiner*
Restore	*Rétablir, restituer*
Retain	*Maintenir*
Revamp	*Retaper, réorganiser, restructurer*
Revise	*Modifier, complètement réviser*
Route (routed)	*Fixer le parcours*
Sales pitch	*Argumentaire de vente*
Schedule	*Établir un programme, programmer, planifier un l'échéancier*
Secure (secured)	*Assurer, garantir*
Semi-colon	*Point virgule*
Sense	*Sentir, ressentir*
Setback	*Échec, un pas en arrière*
Shortlist	*Retenir une candidature*
Slick	*Qui à la parole facile,*
Spacing	*Interligne*
Spearhead	*Être le fer de lance d'un projet*
Stack up	*Empiler*
Stalemate	*Impasse*
Staying within budget	*Ne pas dépasser le budget*
Straighten out	*Régler, tirer au clair*
Streamline	*Rationaliser, rendre plus efficace un système ou opération*
Tackle (a problem)	*S'attaquer (à un problème)*
Take over	*Prendre la responsabilité, prendre la relève, assumer la responsabilité*
Taking the floor	*Prendre la parole*
Train	*Former*
Traineeship	*Stage (en britannique)*
Trim	*Réduire, 'tailler'*
Undertake	*Entreprendre (attention ! car undertaker veut dire croque-morts en anglais)*

Upfront	*Franc, direct, apparent, explicite*
Upgrade	*Hausser le niveau, la qualité*
Weeding out	*Supprimer, faire une sélection qui supprime 'des mauvaise herbes'*
Well argued policy statements	*Déclaration de politique bien argumentée*
Winning bids	*Proposition qui l'emporte, soumission gagnante, (rédiger une soumission à un appel d'offre qui est retenue*
Winning people's cooperation	*Gagner la confiance des gens, leur collaboration, leur adhésions*

Traduction de
'Adjectives to describe what kind of person you are'

Able to take stress	*Efficace sous le stress*
Aggressive	*Accrocheur, offensif*
Analytic	*Analytique*
Assertive	*Assuré*
Capable	*Capable, habile, compétent*
Careful	*Consciencieux*
Cautious	*Prudent*
Cheerful	*Attrayant, joyeux*
Considerate	*Prévenant*
Creative	*Novateur*
Curious	*Curieux*
Dedicated	*Dévoué, consciencieux*
Demanding	*Exigent*
Dependable	*Sûr, fiable, digne de confiance*
Determined	*Décidé, résolu*
Diligent	*Assidu*
Easy-going	*Facile à vivre*
Effective	*Efficace, décisif (accent sur résultats)*
Efficient	*Efficace, compétent (accent sur process)*
Energetic	*Vigoureux, énergique*
Enterprising	*Audacieux*
Fast	*Rapide*
Flexible	*Souple, maniable*
Friendly	*Accueillant*

Goal-oriented	*Ambitieux, focalisé sur le résultat*
Go-getting	*Motivé, plein d'initiative*
Hard-working	*Travailleur*
Helpful	*Serviable, efficace*
Honest	*Loyal, intègre*
Humorous	*Humoristique, amusant*
Imaginative	*Imaginatif*
Insightful	*Perspicace*
Intellectual	*Intellectuel*
Intelligent	*Intelligent*
Natural	*Naturel*
Observant	*Perspicace*
Organized	*Méthodique*
Patient	*Endurant, patient*
Performance-oriented	*Visant le rendement*
Persistent	*Obstiné, tenace*
Persuasive	*Convaincant*
Practical	*Pratique*
Precise	*Précis, méticuleux*
Ready and willing	*Volontaire, toujours prêt*
Resourceful	*Ingénieux, débrouillard*
Responsible	*Fiable, sûr, sérieux*
Risk-taking	*Ayant le goût du risque, entreprenant*
Self-confident	*Sûr de soi, confiant*
Self-starting	*Motivé, plein d'initiative*
Sensitive	*Sensible*
Sincere	*Sincère*
Straightforward	*Franc, honnête*
Street-smart	*Averti, expérimenté*
Supportive	*Qui donne son soutien, d'un grand secours*
Thorough	*Approfondi, faisant les choses à fonds, rigoureux*
Thoughtful	*Réfléchi*
Warm	*Chaleureux*